WRIGHT FAMILY PERSONAL PROPERTY TAX LISTS

1809-1850

NELSON COUNTY
VIRGINIA

Robert N. Grant

HERITAGE BOOKS
2009

HERITAGE BOOKS
AN IMPRINT OF HERITAGE BOOKS, INC.

Books, CDs, and more—Worldwide

For our listing of thousands of titles see our website
at
www.HeritageBooks.com

Published 2009 by
HERITAGE BOOKS, INC.
Publishing Division
100 Railroad Ave. #104
Westminster, Maryland 21157

Copyright © 2009 Robert N. Grant

All rights reserved. No part of this book may be reproduced or transmitted in any form or by any means, electronic or mechanical, including photocopying, recording or by any information storage and retrieval system without written permission from the author, except for the inclusion of brief quotations in a review.

International Standard Book Numbers
Paperbound: 978-0-7884-4937-6
Clothbound: 978-0-7884-8161-1

WRIGHT FAMILY

PERSONAL PROPERTY TAX LISTS

1809 TO 1850

NELSON COUNTY, VIRGINIA

Revised as of September 29, 2008

© 2008, Robert N. Grant
1437(091908)

Introduction To Appendix: Personal Property Tax Records, Nelson County, Virginia

This document is an appendix to a larger work titled Sorting Some Of The Wrights Of Southern Virginia. The work is divided into parts for each family of Wrights that has been researched. Each part is divided into two sections; the first section is text discussing the family and the evidence supporting the relationships and the second section is a descendants chart summarizing the relationships and information known about each individual.

The appendices to the work (of which this document is one) present source records for persons named Wright by county and by type of record with the identification of the person named and their Wright ancestors to the extent known.

The source for the records listed in this appendix is the following:

1) Nelson County, Virginia, Personal Property Tax Lists, available from the Virginia State Library & Archives, 11th & Capitol Streets, Richmond, Virginia 23219.

The identification of a person or their ancestor by year and county indicates their year of death and county of residence at death. For example, "1763 Thomas Wright of Bedford County" indicates that this was the Thomas Wright who died in 1763 in Bedford County. If no state is listed after the county, the state is Virginia; counties in states other than Virginia will have a state listed after the county, as in "1876 William S. Wright of Highland County, Ohio".

A parenthetical after the name indicates an identification of the person when a place of death is not yet known, as in "John Wright (Goochland County Carpenter)". A county in parentheses after the name indicates the county with which that person was most identified when no evidence of the place of death has yet been found, as in "Grief Wright (Bedford County)".

All or portions of the text and descendants charts for each Wright family identified are available from the author:

Robert N. Grant
15 Campo Bello Court		(H) 650-854-0895
Menlo Park, California 94025	(O) 650-614-3800

This is a work in process and I would be most interested in receiving additional information about any of the persons identified in these records in order to correct any errors or expand on the information given.

1809 PERSONAL PROPERTY TAX LIST

NELSON COUNTY, VIRGINIA

Appendix: Nelson County, Virginia, 1809 Personal Property Tax List:

List of Taxable _erty in the County of Nelson 1809	Whites above 16	Blacks above 16	Stud Horses rates of Covering 1 Mare the Season Carriages Seins, &c		Identification
Jno Wright (Son Robt)	1	1		2	John Wright, son of 1816 Robert Wright of Nelson County and grandson of William Wright (Amherst County)
Jno Wright (Son Jas)	2	1		1	John Wright, son of 1839 James Wright of Nelson County and grandson of William Wright (Amherst County)
Robt Wright	1	3	1	5	1816 Robert Wright of Nelson County, son of William Wright (Amherst County)
Jno. Wright (Watr)	2			3	John Wright, son of 1776 Augustine Wright of Amherst County
Austin Wright	1		2		1838 Augustine Wright of Nelson County, son of 1776 Augustine Wright of Amherst County
Jas. Wright (Son Jas)	1			1	James Wright, son of 1839 James Wright of Nelson County and grandson of William Wright (Amherst County)
Wm. Wright	1	3	1	7	William Wright, Jr., son of William Wright (Amherst County)
Andrew Wright	1	2	1	4	1816 Andrew Wright of Nelson County, son of William Wright (Amherst County)
Benj. Wright	1				1861 Benjamin Wright of Nelson County, son of 1816 Andrew Wright of Nelson County and grandson of William Wright (Amherst County)
Alxr. Wright	1			9	1861 Alexander Wright of Holt County, Missouri, son of 1839 James Wright of Nelson County and grandson of William Wright (Amherst County)
Archillis Wright	2	4		3	1825 Achilles Wright of Oldham County, Kentucky

1437(091908)

Appendix: Nelson County, Virginia, 1809 Personal Property Tax List:

List of Taxable _erty in the County of Nelson 1809	Whites above 16	Blacks above 16	Stud Horses rates of Covering 1 Mare the Season Carriages Seins, &c		Identification
Jessee Wright	1	3		3	1850 Jesse Wright of Nelson County, son of 1799 Benjamin Wright of Amherst County and grandson of 1767 Frances Wright of Amherst County
Jas Wright Senr	1	4		6	1839 James Wright of Nelson County, son of William Wright (Amherst County)
Moses Wright	1				

1810 PERSONAL PROPERTY TAX LIST

NELSON COUNTY, VIRGINIA

Appendix: Nelson County, Virginia, 1810 Personal Property Tax List:

A List of Taxable property in the County of Nelson 1810	White Males over 16 years	Blacks over 16 years	Blacks between 12 and 16 years	Horses Mares Colts & Mules	Stud Horses at the rate of one mare the Season	Riding Carriages and Seins	Identification

[No Wrights listed, W's missing]

1811 PERSONAL PROPERTY TAX LIST

NELSON COUNTY, VIRGINIA

Appendix: Nelson County, Virginia, 1811 Personal Property Tax List:

A List of Taxable property in Nelson County 1811	Whites above 16 years of age	Blacks over 16 years of age	Blacks between 12 and 16 years of age	Horses Mares Colts and Mules	Stud Horses at the rate of covering one mare the Season	Riding Carriages and Seins	Identification
Andrew Wright	1	2	2	4			1816 Andrew Wright of Nelson County, son of William Wright (Amherst County)
Robert Wright	1	4	1	4			1816 Robert Wright of Nelson County, son of William Wright (Amherst County)
Alexr. Wright	1			2			1861 Alexander Wright of Holt County, Missouri, son of 1839 James Wright of Nelson County and grandson of William Wright (Amherst County)
Jono. Wright (SR)	1	1		2			John Wright, son of 1816 Robert Wright of Nelson County and grandson of William Wright (Amherst County)
Benjn Wright	1	2					1861 Benjamin Wright of Nelson County, son of 1816 Andrew Wright of Nelson County and grandson of William Wright (Amherst County)
Jas Wright (Son James)	1						James Wright, son of 1839 James Wright of Nelson County and grandson of William Wright (Amherst County)
Jas Wright	1	4		4			1839 James Wright of Nelson County, son of William Wright (Amherst County)
Jno. Wright (Water)	2			1			John Wright, son of 1776 Augustine Wright of Amherst County
Jesse Wright	1	2		2			1850 Jesse Wright of Nelson County, son of 1799 Benjamin Wright of Amherst County and grandson of 1767 Frances Wright of Amherst County

Appendix: Nelson County, Virginia, 1811 Personal Property Tax List:

A List of Taxable property in Nelson County 1811	Whites above 16 years of age	Blacks over 16 years of age	Blacks between 12 and 16 years of age	Horses Mares Colts and Mules	Stud Horses at the rate of covering one mare the Season	Riding Carriages and Seins	Identification
Moses Wright	1						
Permenos Wright	1			1			Parmenos Wright

1812 PERSONAL PROPERTY TAX LIST

NELSON COUNTY, VIRGINIA

Appendix: Nelson County, Virginia, 1812 Personal Property Tax List:

A list of Taxable Property in the County of Nelson February 28th 1812	White Males above 16 years	Blacks above 16 years	Blacks between 12 & 16	Horses Mares Colts & mules	Stud Horses at the rate of covering 1 mare the Season	Riding Carriages and Seins	Identification
John Wright (Black)	1	1	1	2			John Wright, son of 1839 James Wright of Nelson County and grandson of William Wright (Amherst County)
Robert Wright	1	4	1	4			1816 Robert Wright of Nelson County, son of William Wright (Amherst County)
Andrew Wright	1	2	2	3			1816 Andrew Wright of Nelson County, son of William Wright (Amherst County)
John Wright (S to R)	1	1		1			John Wright, son of 1816 Robert Wright of Nelson County and grandson of William Wright (Amherst County)
Alec Wright	1			2			1861 Alexander Wright of Holt County, Missouri, son of 1839 James Wright of Nelson County and grandson of William Wright (Amherst County)
Benj Wright	1			1			1861 Benjamin Wright of Nelson County, son of 1816 Andrew Wright of Nelson County and grandson of William Wright (Amherst County)
John Wright (wat)	2	1		1			John Wright, son of 1776 Augustine Wright of Amherst County
William Wright (S to J)	0	1					Probably William Wright, son of John Wright and grandson of 1776 Augustine Wright of Amherst County
Austin Wright	1	1					1838 Augustine Wright of Nelson County, son of 1776 Augustine Wright of Amherst County

Appendix: Nelson County, Virginia, 1812 Personal Property Tax List:

A list of Taxable Property in the County of Nelson February 28th 1812	White Males above 16 years	Blacks above 16 years	Blacks between 12 & 16	Horses Mares Colts & mules	Stud Horses at the rate of covering 1 mare the Season	Riding Carriages and Seins	Identification
William Wright (TR)	0	1					William Wright, son of 1776 Augustine Wright of Amherst County
William Wright	1	3	1	4			William Wright, Jr., son of William Wright (Amherst County)
Jesse Wright	1	3		2			1850 Jesse Wright of Nelson County, son of 1799 Benjamin Wright of Amherst County and grandson of 1767 Frances Wright of Amherst County
Landon Wright	1						
Parmenos Wright	1		1				Parmenos Wright
Moses Wright	2						

1813 PERSONAL PROPERTY TAX LIST

NELSON COUNTY, VIRGINIA

Appendix: Nelson County, Virginia, 1813 Personal Property Tax List:

A List of Taxable Property in the County of Nelson 28th Feby 1813	Whites over 16	Blacks over 16 years of age	Blacks between 12 & 16 years of age	horses mares mules & Colts	Stud Horses at the rate of covering one mare by the Season	Riding Carriages sei__ & __ at___	Identification
Moses Wright	1						
Thos Wright	1						
Wm Wright	1	4	1	4			William Wright, Jr., son of William Wright (Amherst County)
Austin Wright	1	1					1838 Augustine Wright of Nelson County, son of 1776 Augustine Wright of Amherst County
Andrew Wright	1	2	2	3			1816 Andrew Wright of Nelson County, son of William Wright (Amherst County)
Ben Wright	1	1		2			1861 Benjamin Wright of Nelson County, son of 1816 Andrew Wright of Nelson County and grandson of William Wright (Amherst County)
Wm Wright		1		1			
Jesse Wright	1	3		3			1850 Jesse Wright of Nelson County, son of 1799 Benjamin Wright of Amherst County and grandson of 1767 Frances Wright of Amherst County
Alex. Wright	1			2			1861 Alexander Wright of Holt County, Missouri, son of 1839 James Wright of Nelson County and grandson of William Wright (Amherst County)
James Wright	1	3		4			1839 James Wright of Nelson County and grandson of William Wright (Amherst County)

Appendix: Nelson County, Virginia, 1813 Personal Property Tax List:

A List of Taxable Property in the County of Nelson 28th Feby 1813	Whites over 16	Blacks over 16 years of age	Blacks between 12 & 16 years of age	horses mares mules & Colts	Stud Horses at the rate of covering one mare by the Season	Riding Carriages sei__ & __ at___	Identification
Nelson Wright	1			1			Nelson Wright, son of ____ Wright, grandson of 1839 James Wright of Nelson County, and great grandson of William Wright (Amherst County)
James Wright	1						James Wright, son of 1839 James Wright of Nelson County and grandson of William Wright (Amherst County)
Ro. Wright	1	4	1	3			1816 Robert Wright of Nelson County, son of William Wright (Amherst County)
Jno Wright (SR)	1	1		1			John Wright, son of 1816 Robert Wright of Nelson County and grandson of William Wright (Amherst County)
Jno. Wright (BS)	1	1	1	2			John Wright, son of 1839 James Wright of Nelson County and grandson of William Wright (Amherst County)
Jno Wright	1						

1814 PERSONAL PROPERTY TAX LIST

NELSON COUNTY, VIRGINIA

Appendix: Nelson County, Virginia, 1814 Personal Property Tax List:

A list of Taxable property in the County of Nelson 28th February 1814	Whites over 16 years old	Blacks over 16 years old	Blacks between 12 & 16 years old	horses mares mules & colts	Stud Horses at the rate of covering 1 mare by the Season	Riding Carriages mills __ & Tanyards &c	Identification
Jno Wright BS	1	2		1			John Wright, son of 1839 James Wright of Nelson County and grandson of William Wright (Amherst County)
Nelson Wright	1			1			Nelson Wright, son of ____ Wright, grandson of 1839 James Wright of Nelson County, and great grandson of William Wright (Amherst County)
James Wright	1						James Wright, son of 1839 James Wright of Nelson County and grandson of William Wright (Amherst County)
Wm Wright	1	4	1	3			William Wright, Jr., son of William Wright (Amherst County)
Robert Wright	1	4	1	4			1816 Robert Wright of Nelson County, son of William Wright (Amherst County)
John Wright	1	1		2			
Austin Wright	1	1					1838 Augustine Wright of Nelson County, son of 1776 Augustine Wright of Amherst County
Parmenos Wright	1			2			Parmenos Wright
Alex Wright	1			2			1861 Alexander Wright of Holt County, Missouri, son of 1839 James Wright of Nelson County and grandson of William Wright (Amherst County)
James Wright	1	2		11			1839 James Wright of Nelson County, son of William Wright (Amherst County)

1437(091908)

Appendix: Nelson County, Virginia, 1814 Personal Property Tax List:

A list of Taxable property in the County of Nelson 28th February 1814	Whites over 16 years old	Blacks over 16 years old	Blacks between 12 & 16 years old	horses mares mules & colts	Stud Horses at the rate of covering 1 mare by the Season	Riding Carriages mills __ & Tanyards &c	Identification
Wm Wright				1			
Ben Wright	1			1			1861 Benjamin Wright of Nelson County, son of 1816 Andrew Wright of Nelson County and grandson of William Wright (Amherst County)
John Wright	1						
Andrew Wright	1	3	2	4			1816 Andrew Wright of Nelson County, son of William Wright (Amherst County)
Jesse Wright	1	3		3			1850 Jesse Wright of Nelson County, son of 1799 Benjamin Wright of Amherst County and grandson of 1767 Frances Wright of Amherst County
Thos Wright	1						

1815 PERSONAL PROPERTY TAX LIST

NELSON COUNTY, VIRGINIA

Appendix: Nelson County, Virginia, 1815 Personal Property Tax List:

District of Landon Cabell:

Date of receiving list Individuals	Persons names charged with Taxable property	No white Tythes above 16 years old	Slaves between 12 years old	Slaves above 12 years old	horses asses mares mules & colts	No heads of cattle	Stud horses	the rate of covering one mare by the Season	Two wheel riding carriages	carriages Phaeton & stage waggons (none)	public stages (none)	All other four wheel riding carriages	Mills	_ & Ferries
March 4	Wm Wright	1		5	3	7								
March 4	Ben Wright	1			1	2								
March 8	Andrew Wright	1		4	4	9								
March 21	Jno Wright (W)	2				2								
March 21	Wm Wright	1												
March 21	Austin Wright	1		1										
March 23	Jno Wright (BS)	1		2	2									
March 24	Ro. Wright	1	1	5	2	6								
March 24	Jas. Wright	1		2	4	8								

Appendix: Nelson County, Virginia, 1815 Personal Property Tax List:

District of Landon Cabell:

Persons names charged with Taxable property [continued from prior page]	Tanyards	Free negros & molattoes above 16 years old & under 45	silver or ___ch- back	Watches Single cased Gold	Double cased Gold	exceed- ing $300 in value			Clocks of Wood without a case	Clocks wood with a case	works princi- pally metal	of value between 50 & 100$	of value 200 & upwards	Printers & their Personal sub- scriptions to their papers (none)
Wm Wright														
Ben Wright														
Andrew Wright														
Jno Wright (W)														
Wm Wright														
Austin Wright														
Jno Wright (BS)														
Ro. Wright														
Jas. Wright														

1437(091908)

Appendix: Nelson County, Virginia, 1815 Personal Property Tax List:

District of Landon Cabell:

Persons names charged with Taxable property [continued from prior page]	coal pits (none)	Bureaus, secretaries or book cases in whole or in part mahogany	Bureaus, secretaries or book cases of any other wood than mahogany	Chest of draws with or without a desk in whole or in part mahogany	Chest of draws with or without a desk of any other wood than mahogany	Ce_ or sideboard with drawers or doors of less than $100 in value	Ce_ or sideboard with draws or doors of $100 in value or upwards	Wardrobe or clothes press in whole or in part mahogany	Wardrobe or clothes press of any other wood than mahogany	Dining tables or separate ____ thereof in whole or in part mahogany
Wm Wright										
Ben Wright										
Andrew Wright										
Jno Wright (W)										
Wm Wright										
Austin Wright										
Jno Wright (BS)										
Ro. Wright										
Jas. Wright										

Appendix: Nelson County, Virginia, 1815 Personal Property Tax List:

District of Landon Cabell:

Persons names charged with Taxable property [continued from prior page]	Sideboards without drawers or doors Tea tables & card tables in whole or in part mahogany	Bedsteads in whole or in part Mahoganey	____ or sophas in whole or in part mahogany	Settees or sophas in whole or in part of bamboo or ____	Settees or sophas with bottoms of rush, straw or __ ____ of any bamboo or cane in any part & with bottoms neither rush flax or Straw	Chairs in whole or in part mahogany, bamboo or cane or with rush straw or flag bottom & ornamented with gold or Silver leaf	Chairs ornamented with gold or Silver leaf but without mahogany in part & housing bottoms with neither rush flax nor straw
Wm Wright							
Ben Wright							
Andrew Wright							
Jno Wright (W)							
Wm Wright							
Austin Wright							
Jno Wright (BS)							
Ro. Wright							
Jas. Wright							

1437(091908)

Appendix: Nelson County, Virginia, 1815 Personal Property Tax List:

District of Landon Cabell:

Persons names charged with Taxable property [continued from prior page]	Carpets above 20 & not exceeding 50$ in value	Carpets of $50 & less than $100 in value	Carpets of the value of $100 & upwards	The curtains of each window where the same are of calico, muselin dimity not manufactured in the family	The curtains of each window where the same are of worsted Silk or Satan	Vin_ blinds with the apointment of any house	Portraits in oil	Portraits in crayon	Pictures, prints or engravings above 12 Inches in breadth their frames inclusive
Wm Wright									
Ben Wright									
Andrew Wright									
Jno Wright (W)									
Wm Wright									
Austin Wright									
Jno Wright (BS)									
Ro. Wright									
Jas. Wright									

Appendix: Nelson County, Virginia, 1815 Personal Property Tax List:

District of Landon Cabell:

Persons names charged with Taxable property [continued from prior page]	Pictures, engravings or prints of 12 Inches in breadth or under when enclosed in a gilt frame	Mirrors or looking Glasses of or above 5 feet in length	Mirrors or looking glasses of 4 & under 5 feet in length exclusive of frames	Mirrors or looking glasses of 3 & under 4 feet in length exclusive of their frames	Mirrors or looking glasses of ones under 2 feet, if enclosed in a gilt frame	Pianos, Harpsichords, organs or harps under $300 in value	Pianos, harpsichords organs or harps of the value of $300 or upwards	Silver Coffee pots and Urns	plated Urns	plated coffee pots & Tea pots
Wm Wright										
Ben Wright										
Andrew Wright										
Jno Wright (W)										
Wm Wright										
Austin Wright										
Jno Wright (BS)										
Ro. Wright										
Jas. Wright										

Appendix: Nelson County, Virginia, 1815 Personal Property Tax List:

District of Landon Cabell:

Persons names charged with Taxable property [continued from prior page]	Silver and cut glass candlesticks lamp, chandeliers, ____ & G_____	plated candle- sticks lamps chandeliers ____ & _____	Cut glass decanters, pitchers, bowls, Goblets, wash basons, stands &c	Silver pitchers, Tankards, cups, saucers & waiters	_____	Identification
Wm Wright						William Wright, Jr., son of William Wright (Amherst County)
Ben Wright						1861 Benjamin Wright of Nelson County, son of 1816 Andrew Wright of Nelson County and grandson of William Wright (Amherst County)
Andrew Wright						1816 Andrew Wright of Nelson County, son of William Wright (Amherst County)
Jno Wright (W)						John Wright, son of 1776 Augustine Wright of Amherst County
Wm Wright						Probably William Wright, son of John Wright and grandson of 1776 Augustine Wright of Amherst County
Austin Wright						1838 Austin Wright of Nelson County, son of 1776 Augustine Wright of Amherst County
Jno Wright (BS)						John Wright, son of 1839 James Wright of Nelson County and grandson of William Wright (Amherst County)
Ro. Wright						1816 Robert Wright of Nelson County, son of William Wright (Amherst County)
Jas. Wright						1839 James Wright of Nelson County, son of William Wright (Amherst County)

Appendix: Nelson County, Virginia, 1815 Personal Property Tax List:

District of Landon Cabell:

Date of receiving list Individuals	Persons names charged with Taxable property	No white Tythes above 16 years old	Slaves between 12 years old	Slaves above 12 years old	horses asses mares mules & colts	No heads of cattle	Stud horses	the rate of covering one mare by the Season	Two wheel riding carriages	carriages Phaeton & stage waggons (none)	public stages (none)	All other four wheel riding carriages	Mills	& Ferries
March 27	Jas. Wright	1			1									
March 27	Austin Wright	1		2										
March 27	Nelson Wright	1			1									
March 27	Alex. Wright	1			3	5								
Apl 4	Jno Wright (SR)	1	1	1	6	6								
Apl 28	Jesse Wright	1	1	3	3	13								

Appendix: Nelson County, Virginia, 1815 Personal Property Tax List:

District of Landon Cabell:

Persons names charged with Taxable property [continued from prior page]	Tanyards	Free negros & molattoes above 16 years old & under 45	Watches						Clocks					Printers & their Personal sub- scriptions to their papers (none)
			silver or ___ch- back	Single cased Gold	Double cased Gold	exceed- ing $300 in value	___	___	Clocks of Wood without a case	Clocks wood with a case	works princi- pally metal	of value between 50 & 100$	of value 200 & upwards	
Jas. Wright														
Austin Wright														
Nelson Wright														
Alex. Wright														
Jno Wright (SR)														
Jesse Wright														

1437(091908)

Appendix: Nelson County, Virginia, 1815 Personal Property Tax List:

District of Landon Cabell:

Persons names charged with Taxable property [continued from prior page]	coal pits (none)	Bureaus, secretaries or book cases in whole or in part mahogany	Bureaus, secretaries or book cases of any other wood than mahogany	Chest of draws with or without a desk in whole or in part mahogany	Chest of draws with or without a desk of any other wood than mahogany	Ce_ or sideboard with drawers or doors of less than $100 in value	Ce_ or sideboard with draws or doors of $100 in value or upwards	Wardrobe or clothes press in whole or in part mahogany	Wardrobe or clothes press of any other wood than mahogany	Dining tables or separate ____ thereof in whole or in part mahogany
Jas. Wright										
Austin Wright										
Nelson Wright										
Alex. Wright										
Jno Wright (SR)										
Jesse Wright										

1437(091908)

Appendix: Nelson County, Virginia, 1815 Personal Property Tax List:

District of Landon Cabell:

Persons names charged with Taxable property [continued from prior page]	Sideboards without drawers or doors Tea tables & card tables in whole or in part mahogany	Bedsteads in whole or in part Mahoganey	____ or sophas in whole or in part mahogany	Settees or sophas in whole or in part of bamboo or ____	Settees or sophas with bottoms of rush, straw or __ ____ of any bamboo or cane in any part & with bottoms neither rush flax or Straw	Chairs in whole or in part mahogany, bamboo or cane or with rush straw or flag bottom & ornamented with gold or Silver leaf	Chairs ornamented with gold or Silver leaf but without mahogany in part & housing bottoms with neither rush flax nor straw
Jas. Wright							
Austin Wright							
Nelson Wright							
Alex. Wright							
Jno Wright (SR)							
Jesse Wright							

Appendix: Nelson County, Virginia, 1815 Personal Property Tax List:

District of Landon Cabell:

Persons names charged with Taxable property [continued from prior page]	Carpets above 20 & not exceeding 50$ in value	Carpets of $50 & less than $100 in value	Carpets of the value of $100 & upwards	The curtains of each window where the same are of calico, muselin dimity not manufactured in the family	The curtains of each window where the same are of worsted Silk or Satan	Vin_ blinds with the apointment of any house	Portraits in oil	Portraits in crayon	Pictures, prints or engravings above 12 Inches in breadth their frames inclusive
Jas. Wright									
Austin Wright									
Nelson Wright									
Alex. Wright									
Jno Wright (SR)									
Jesse Wright									

1437(091908)

Appendix: Nelson County, Virginia, 1815 Personal Property Tax List:

District of Landon Cabell:

Persons names charged with Taxable property [continued from prior page]	Pictures, engravings or prints of 12 Inches in breadth or under when enclosed in a gilt frame	Mirrors or looking Glasses of or above 5 feet in length	Mirrors or looking glasses of 4 & under 5 feet in length exclusive of frames	Mirrors or looking glasses of 3 & under 4 feet in length exclusive of their frames	Mirrors or looking glasses of ones under 2 feet, if enclosed in a gilt frame	Pianos, Harpsichords, organs or harps under $300 in value	Pianos, harpsichords organs or harps of the value of $300 or upwards	Silver Coffee pots and Urns	plated Urns	plated coffee pots & Tea pots
Jas. Wright										
Austin Wright										
Nelson Wright										
Alex. Wright										
Jno Wright (SR)										
Jesse Wright										

Appendix: Nelson County, Virginia, 1815 Personal Property Tax List:

District of Landon Cabell:

Persons names charged with Taxable property [continued from prior page]	Silver and cut glass candlesticks lamp, chandeliers, ____ & G	plated candlesticks lamps chandeliers ____ & &	Cut glass decanters, pitchers, bowls, Goblets, wash basons, stands &c	Silver pitchers, Tankards, cups, saucers & waiters		Identification
Jas. Wright						1839 James Wright of Nelson County, son of William Wright (Amherst County)
Austin Wright						1838 Augustine Wright of Nelson County, son of 1776 Augustine Wright of Amherst County
Nelson Wright						Nelson Wright, son of ____ Wright, grandson of 1839 James Wright of Nelson County, and great grandson of William Wright (Amherst County)
Alex. Wright						1861 Alexander Wright of Holt County, Missouri, son of 1839 James Wright of Nelson County and grandson of William Wright (Amherst County)
Jno Wright (SR)						John Wright, son of 1816 Robert Wright of Nelson County and grandson of William Wright (Amherst County)
Jesse Wright						1850 Jesse Wright of Nelson County, son of 1799 Benjamin Wright of Amherst County and grandson of 1767 Frances Wright of Amherst County

1437(091908)

1816 PERSONAL PROPERTY TAX LIST

NELSON COUNTY, VIRGINIA

Appendix: Nelson County, Virginia, 1816 Personal Property Tax List:

Date of receiving List	Persons Names	White Tythes above 16	Negroes between 12 & 16	Negroes above 16	Horses Asses Mares Mules, & Colts	Stud Horses & their Rate of covering one mare by the Season	Two wheeled Riding Carriages	Phaeton & Stage Waggons	All other Riding Carriages	Seines	Amount of Tax
Feby 23	John Wright	1									
Apl. 1	Benj Wright	1		2							1.40
Apl. 1	Wm Wright	1		4	3						3.24
Apl. 1	Nelson Wright	1			1						.18
Apl. 2	Jesse Wright	1		3	4						2.82
Apl 18	Landon Wright	1									
Apl 22	Austin Wright Jr	1									
Apl 22	Wm Wright (P)		1	1							
Apl. 27	Austin Wright	1	1	2							2.10
Apl 29	Andrew Wright	1		4	6						3.85
Apl 29	Jno Wright SR	1	1	1	5						.30
Apl 29	_ Wright	1	1	2	3						4.94
May 6	Alex Wright	1			3						.54
May 27	James Wright	1		2	4						2.12
May 27	John Wright	1		3	1						1.58

Appendix: Nelson County, Virginia, 1816 Personal Property Tax List:

Persons Names [Continued from previous page]	Identification
John Wright	
Benj Wright	1861 Benjamin Wright of Nelson County, son of 1816 Andrew Wright of Nelson County and grandson of William Wright (Amherst County)
Wm Wright	William Wright, Jr., son of William Wright (Amherst County)
Nelson Wright	Nelson Wright, son of ____ Wright, grandson of 1839 James Wright of Nelson County, and great grandson of William Wright (Amherst County)
Jesse Wright	1850 Jesse Wright of Nelson County, son of 1799 Benjamin Wright of Amherst County and grandson of 1767 Frances Wright of Amherst County
Landon Wright	
Austin Wright Jr	
Wm Wright (P)	1851 William Wright of Amherst County
Austin Wright	1838 Augustine Wright of Nelson County, son of 1776 Augustine Wright of Amherst County
Andrew Wright	1816 Andrew Wright of Nelson County, son of William Wright (Amherst County)
Jno Wright SR	John Wright, son of 1816 Robert Wright of Nelson County and grandson of William Wright (Amherst County)
_ Wright	
Alex Wright	
James Wright	1839 James Wright of Nelson County, son of William Wright (Amherst County)
John Wright	John Wright, son of 1839 James Wright of Nelson County and grandson of William Wright (Amherst County)

1817 PERSONAL PROPERTY TAX LIST

NELSON COUNTY, VIRGINIA

Appendix: Nelson County, Virginia, 1817 Personal Property Tax List:

Date of receiving List	Persons Names	White tithes above 16	Negroes between 12 & 16	Negroes above 16	Horses asses mares mules, & colts	___ & their Rate of covering Season	___ Riding Carriages	___	___
	John Wright (S to Ro)	2	1	2	6				3.18
	James Wright	1		2	3				1.94
	William Wright (P)			1	1				3.62
	Benj. Wright	1		1	1				
	[illegible]								
	William Wright	1		4	4				3.52
	[illegible]								
	Austin Wright	1	1		2				2.16
	Jesse Wright	2	1	3	5				3.70

Appendix: Nelson County, Virginia, 1817 Personal Property Tax List:

Persons Names [Continued from previous page]	Identification
John Wright (S to Ro)	John Wright, son of 1816 Robert Wright of Nelson County and grandson of William Wright (Amherst County)
James Wright	1839 James Wright of Nelson County, son of William Wright (Amherst County)
William Wright (P)	1851 William Wright of Amherst County
Benj. Wright	1861 Benjamin Wright of Nelson County, son of 1816 Andrew Wright of Nelson County and grandson of William Wright (Amherst County)
[illegible]	
William Wright	William Wright, Jr., son of William Wright (Amherst County)
[illegible]	
Austin Wright	1838 Augustine Wright of Nelson County, son of 1776 Augustine Wright of Amherst County
Jesse Wright	1850 Jesse Wright of Nelson County, son of 1799 Benjamin Wright of Amherst County and grandson of 1767 Frances Wright of Amherst County

1818 PERSONAL PROPERTY TAX LIST

NELSON COUNTY, VIRGINIA

Appendix: Nelson County, Virginia, 1818 Personal Property Tax List:

Date of receiving List	Persons Names	White Tythes above 16	Negroes between 12 & 16	Negroes above 16	horses asses mares mules and colts	Stud horses and the rate of covering one mare by the Season	two wheeled riding carriages	Phaetons & Stage Waggons	all other riding Carriages	Seines	Amount of Tax
	Austin Wright jr	1									
	Jno Wright	1									
	Margret Wright			1							.70
	Wm Wright	1		3	4						2.82
	Benj. Wright	1		3	13						4.44
	Lucy Wright			1	4						1.42
	Alexander Wright	1			2						.36
	Jno Wright (Wag)	2		2	3						1.94
	Wm Wright	1		1	1						.88
	James Wright	1	1	2	4						2.82
	Westley Wright	1									
	John Wright (Bla)	1	1	2	1						2.28
	Austin Wright	1	1	6	3						5.44
	Jesse Wright	2	1	3	5						3.70

Appendix: Nelson County, Virginia, 1818 Personal Property Tax List:

Persons Names [Continued from previous page	Identification
Austin Wright jr	
Jno Wright	
Margret Wright	
Wm Wright	William Wright, Jr., son of William Wright (Amherst County)
Benj. Wright	1861 Benjamin Wright of Nelson County, son of 1816 Andrew Wright of Nelson County and grandson of William Wright (Amherst County)
Lucy Wright	Lucy (Childress) Wright, wife of 1816 Andrew Wright of Nelson County, a son of William Wright (Amherst County)
Alexander Wright	1861 Alexander Wright of Holt County, Missouri, son of 1839 James Wright of Nelson County and grandson of William Wright (Amherst County)
Jno Wright (Wag)	
Wm Wright	
James Wright	1839 James Wright of Nelson County, son of William Wright (Amherst County)
Westley Wright	
John Wright (Bla)	John Wright, son of 1839 James Wright of Nelson County and grandson of William Wright (Amherst County)
Austin Wright	1838 Augustine Wright of Nelson County, son of 1776 Augustine Wright of Amherst County
Jesse Wright	1850 Jesse Wright of Nelson County, son of 1799 Benjamin Wright of Amherst County and grandson of 1767 Frances Wright of Amherst County

1819 PERSONAL PROPERTY TAX LIST

NELSON COUNTY, VIRGINIA

1819 List not located

1820 PERSONAL PROPERTY TAX LIST

NELSON COUNTY, VIRGINIA

Appendix: Nelson County, Virginia, 1820 Personal Property Tax List:

Date of Receiving list of Individuals	Persons Names chargeable with tax	Number of white males above 16 years	Blacks above 12 & under 16 years	Blacks above 16 years old	horses mares mules and colts	Ordinary License						
February 4	Benjamin Wright	1		2	4							
February 4	William Wright	1		4	4							
February 28	John Wright	1		7	1							
February 28	Alexander Wright	1			1							
February 28	Nelson Wright	1										
February 28	John Wright (Son of Robert)	1		2	7							
March 17	William Wright (Preacher)	1	1	1	1							
March 27	Austin Wright		2	1	2							
March 29	James Wright	1		3	4							
April 1	George G. Wright	1										
April 24	Jesse Wright	2	1	3	3							

Appendix: Nelson County, Virginia, 1820 Personal Property Tax List:

Persons Names chargeable with tax [continued from prior page]	Sum toal of Taxes	Total amount	Identification
Benjamin Wright	2.12		1861 Benjamin Wright of Nelson County, son of 1816 Andrew Wright of Nelson County and grandson of William Wright (Amherst County)
William Wright	3.32		William Wright, Jr., son of William Wright (Amherst County)
John Wright	1.38		
Alexander Wright	.18		1861 Alexander Wright of Holt County, Missouri, son of 1839 James Wright of Nelson County and grandson of William Wright (Amherst County)
Nelson Wright			Nelson Wright, son of ____ Wright, grandson of 1839 James Wright of Nelson County, and great grandson of William Wright (Amherst County)
John Wright (Son of Robert)	2.66		John Wright, son of 1816 Robert Wright of Nelson County and grandson of William Wright (Amherst County)
William Wright (Preacher)	1.38		1851 William Wright of Amherst County
Austin Wright	2.46		1838 Augustine Wright of Nelson County, son of 1776 Augustine Wright of Amherst County
James Wright	2.82		1839 James Wright of Nelson County, son of William Wright (Amherst County)
George G. Wright			George G. Wright, son of 1850 Jesse Wright of Nelson County, grandson of 1799 Benjamin Wright of Amherst County, and great grandson of 1767 Francis Wright of Amherst County
Jesse Wright	3.70		1850 Jesse Wright of Nelson County, son of 1799 Benjamin Wright of Amherst County and grandson of 1767 Frances Wright of Amherst County

1821 PERSONAL PROPERTY TAX LIST

NELSON COUNTY, VIRGINIA

Appendix: Nelson County, Virginia, 1821 Personal Property Tax List:

	Persons Names Chargeable with Tax	Number of white males above 16 years old	Blacks above 12 years old	Blacks above 16 years old	Horses Mares Colts and Mules	Stud horses and jack asses	Rate of covering p Season	Coaches Charriots & post Chaises	Other riding four wheeled Carriages	Riding Carriages with two wheels	Value of each Carriage
March 26	John Wright (BS)	1		2	1						
March 26	William Wright Senr	1		4	3						
March 26	Benjamin Wright	1		1	1						
April 23	William Wright (Preacher)	1		1	1						
April 23	James Wright	1		3	5						
April 23	George G Wright	1									
April 23	Nelson Wright	1									
April 27	Lucy Wright				2						
May 13	Jesse Wright	2	3	3	7						

Appendix: Nelson County, Virginia, 1821 Personal Property Tax List:

Persons Names Chargeable with Tax [continued from prior page]	Tax on each Carriage D C	Sum total of Taxes D C	Identification
John Wright (BS)		1.19½	John Wright, son of 1839 James Wright of Nelson County and grandson of William Wright (Amherst County)
William Wright Senr		2.52½	William Wright, Jr., son of William Wright (Amherst County)
Benjamin Wright		.66½	1861 Benjamin Wright of Nelson County, son of 1816 Andrew Wright of Nelson County and grandson of William Wright (Amherst County)
William Wright (Preacher)		.66½	1851 William Wright of Amherst County
James Wright		2.26½	1839 James Wright of Nelson County, son of William Wright (Amherst County)
George G Wright			George G. Wright, son of 1850 Jesse Wright of Nelson County, grandson of 1799 Benjamin Wright of Amherst County, and great grandson of 1767 Francis Wright of Amherst County
Nelson Wright			Nelson Wright, son of ____ Wright, grandson of 1839 James Wright of Nelson County, and great grandson of William Wright (Amherst County)
Lucy Wright		.27	Lucy (Childress) Wright, wife of 1816 Andrew Wright of Nelson County, a son of William Wright (Amherst County)
Jesse Wright		4.12½	1850 Jesse Wright of Nelson County, son of 1799 Benjamin Wright of Amherst County and grandson of 1767 Frances Wright of Amherst County

1822 PERSONAL PROPERTY TAX LIST

NELSON COUNTY, VIRGINIA

Appendix: Nelson County, Virginia, 1822 Personal Property Tax List:

District of Nelson Anderson:

Date of receiving list of Individuals	Persons names chargeable with Tax	Number of white males above 16 years	Blacks above 12 and under 16 years old	Blacks above 16 years old	Horses Mares Colts and Mules	Stud horses and Jack Asses	Rate of covering p Season	Coaches Charriots & Post Chaises	Other riding four wheeled Carriages	Value of each Carriage in Dollars	Tax on each Carriage
February 25	John Wright (BS)	1		3	1						
February 25	William Wright	1		3	5						
February 25	William Wright (Preacher)	1	1	1	1						
February 25	Austin Wright	1	1	4	7						
February 25	Benjamin Wright	2		2	1						

Appendix: Nelson County, Virginia, 1822 Personal Property Tax List:

District of Nelson Anderson:

Persons names chargeable with Tax [continued from prior page]	Sum total of Taxes D C	Identification
John Wright (BS)	1.19½	John Wright, son of 1839 James Wright of Nelson County and grandson of William Wright (Amherst County)
William Wright	2.26½	William Wright, Jr., son of William Wright (Amherst County)
William Wright (Preacher)	1.19½	1851 William Wright of Amherst County
Austin Wright	2.92	1838 Augustine Wright of Nelson County, son of 1776 Augustine Wright of Amherst County
Benjamin Wright	1.19½	1861 Benjamin Wright of Nelson County, son of 1816 Andrew Wright of Nelson County and grandson of William Wright (Amherst County)

1823 PERSONAL PROPERTY TAX LIST

NELSON COUNTY, VIRGINIA

Appendix: Nelson County, Virginia, 1823 Personal Property Tax List:

District of Nelson Anderson:

Date of receiving list of Individuals	Persons names chargeable with tax	Blacks above 12 years old	Blacks above 16 years old	Horses Mares Colts and Mules	Stud Horses and Jack Asses	Rate of cover-ing p Season	Pleasure Carriages	Value of each Carriage	Tax on each Carriage D C	Sum total of Taxes D C
Feby 22	John Wright		1							.47
Feby 22	Benjamin Wright			1						.12
Feby 25	George G. Wright			1						.12
March 12	Jesse Wright	2	5	5						3.89
March 25	William Wright (Preacher)		1	1						.59
April 24	Lucy Wright			1						.12
April 28	James Wright		4	4						2.36
April 28	William Wright		3	3						1.77
April 28	Austin Wright	2	7	1						4.35

Appendix: Nelson County, Virginia, 1823 Personal Property Tax List:

District of Nelson Anderson:

Persons names chargeable with tax [continued from prior page]	Identification
John Wright	Probably John Wright, son of 1839 James Wright of Nelson County and grandson of William Wright (Amherst County)
Benjamin Wright	1861 Benjamin Wright of Nelson County, son of 1816 Andrew Wright of Nelson County and grandson of William Wright (Amherst County)
George G. Wright	George G. Wright, son of 1850 Jesse Wright of Nelson County, grandson of 1799 Benjamin Wright of Amherst County, and great grandson of 1767 Francis Wright of Amherst County
Jesse Wright	1850 Jesse Wright of Nelson County, son of 1799 Benjamin Wright of Amherst County and grandson of 1767 Frances Wright of Amherst County
William Wright (Preacher)	1851 William Wright of Amherst County
Lucy Wright	Lucy (Childress) Wright, wife of 1816 Andrew Wright of Nelson County, a son of William Wright (Amherst County)
James Wright	1839 James Wright of Nelson County, son of William Wright (Amherst County)
William Wright	William Wright, Jr., son of William Wright (Amherst County)
Austin Wright	1838 Augustine Wright of Nelson County, son of 1776 Augustine Wright of Amherst County

1824 PERSONAL PROPERTY TAX LIST

NELSON COUNTY, VIRGINIA

Appendix: Nelson County, Virginia, 1824 Personal Property Tax List:

District of Nelson Anderson:

Date of Receiving list of Individuals	Persons names chargeable with tax	Number of white males above 16 years	Blacks above 12 and under 16 years old	Blacks above 16 years old	Horses Mares Colts and Mules	Stud horses and Jack asses	Rate of covering p Season	Coaches Charriots and post Chaises	Other riding four wheeled Carriages	Riding Carriages with two wheels	Value of each Carriage
Feby 23	James Wright	1		4	4						
Mar 22	Benjamin Wright	3		1	1						
Mar 22	William Wright	1		3	2						
Mar 22	John Wright (BS)	1									
Mar 24	William B Wright	1									
May 3	George G. Wright	1			1						
May 3	Jesse Wright	3	1	7	3						
May 26	Austin Wright	1		6	2						

Appendix: Nelson County, Virginia, 1824 Personal Property Tax List:

District of Nelson Anderson:

Persons names chargeable with tax [continued from prior page]	Taxes each Carriage D C	Sum total of taxes D C	Identification
James Wright		2.36	1839 James Wright of Nelson County, son of William Wright (Amherst County)
Benjamin Wright		.59	1861 Benjamin Wright of Nelson County, son of 1816 Andrew Wright of Nelson County and grandson of William Wright (Amherst County)
William Wright			William Wright, Jr., son of William Wright (Amherst County)
John Wright (BS)			John Wright, son of 1839 James Wright of Nelson County and grandson of William Wright (Amherst County)
William B Wright			
George G. Wright		.12	George G. Wright, son of 1850 Jesse Wright of Nelson County, grandson of 1799 Benjamin Wright of Amherst County, and great grandson of 1767 Francis Wright of Amherst County
Jesse Wright		4.12	1850 Jesse Wright of Nelson County, son of 1799 Benjamin Wright of Amherst County and grandson of 1767 Frances Wright of Amherst County
Austin Wright		3.06	1838 Augustine Wright of Nelson County, son of 1776 Augustine Wright of Amherst County

1825 PERSONAL PROPERTY TAX LIST

NELSON COUNTY, VIRGINIA

Appendix: Nelson County, Virginia, 1825 Personal Property Tax List:

District of Nelson Anderson:

Feby 26	George G Wright	1			2							
Feby 28	John Wright (BS)	1										
Feby 28	Benjamin Wright	3		1	1							
Feby 28	Lucy Wright				2							
March 28	William Wright	1		3	2							
March 28	Nelson Wright	1										
April 1	Lunden Wright	1										
April 23	James Wright	1	1	4	5							
April 23	Ellis Wright	1										
May 12	Austin Wright	1		7	2							
May 28	Jesse Wright	3	2	7	2							

Appendix: Nelson County, Virginia, 1825 Personal Property Tax List:

District of Nelson Anderson:

[continued from prior page]			Identification
George G Wright	.24		George G. Wright, son of 1850 Jesse Wright of Nelson County, grandson of 1799 Benjamin Wright of Amherst County, and great grandson of 1767 Francis Wright of Amherst County
John Wright (BS)			John Wright, son of 1839 James Wright of Nelson County and grandson of William Wright (Amherst County)
Benjamin Wright	.59		1861 Benjamin Wright of Nelson County, son of 1816 Andrew Wright of Nelson County and grandson of William Wright (Amherst County)
Lucy Wright	.24		Lucy (Childress) Wright, wife of 1816 Andrew Wright of Nelson County, a son of William Wright (Amherst County)
William Wright	1.65		William Wright, Jr., son of William Wright (Amherst County)
Nelson Wright	3.06		Nelson Wright, son of ____ Wright, grandson of 1839 James Wright of Nelson County, and great grandson of William Wright (Amherst County)
Lunden Wright			
James Wright	2.95		1839 James Wright of Nelson County, son of William Wright (Amherst County)
Ellis Wright			1880 Ellis Wright of Amherst County, son of 1850 Jesse Wright of Nelson County, grandson of 1799 Benjamin Wright of Amherst County, and great grandson of 1767 Francis Wright of Amherst County
Austin Wright	3.53		1838 Augustine Wright of Nelson County, son of 1776 Augustine Wright of Amherst County
Jesse Wright	4.47		1850 Jesse Wright of Nelson County, son of 1799 Benjamin Wright of Amherst County and grandson of 1767 Frances Wright of Amherst County

1826 PERSONAL PROPERTY TAX LIST

NELSON COUNTY, VIRGINIA

Appendix: Nelson County, Virginia, 1826 Personal Property Tax List:

District of Nelson Anderson:

Date of Receiving list _ Individuals	Persons names chargeable with Tax	Number of white males above sixteen years old	Blacks above 12 and under 16 years old	Blacks above 16 years old	Horses Mares Colts and Mules	Stud Horses and Jack Asses	Rate of covering p Season	Coaches Charriots and post Chaises	Other riding four wheeled carriages	Riding Carriages with two wheels	Value of each Carriage
Feby 27	Benjamin Wright	3		1							
Feby 27	Lucy Wright				2						
Feby 27	John Wright (BS)	1		2							
Feby 27	James Wright	1	1	5	5						
Mar 23	Nelson Wright	1									
Mar 27	William Wright	1		3	3						
Mar 28	George G Wright	1			2						
Mar 28	Jesse Wright	3	2	7	3						
Mar 28	Ellis Wright	1									
May 12	Austin Wright	1		6	2						

Appendix: Nelson County, Virginia, 1826 Personal Property Tax List:

District of Nelson Anderson:

Persons names chargeable with Tax [continued from prior page]	Taxes each Carriage	Sum Total of Taxes	Identification
Benjamin Wright		.47	1861 Benjamin Wright of Nelson County, son of 1816 Andrew Wright of Nelson County and grandson of William Wright (Amherst County)
Lucy Wright		.24	Lucy (Childress) Wright, wife of 1816 Andrew Wright of Nelson County, a son of William Wright (Amherst County)
John Wright (BS)		.94	John Wright, son of 1839 James Wright of Nelson County and grandson of William Wright (Amherst County)
James Wright		3.42	1839 James Wright of Nelson County, son of William Wright (Amherst County)
Nelson Wright			Nelson Wright, son of ____ Wright, grandson of 1839 James Wright of Nelson County, and great grandson of William Wright (Amherst County)
William Wright		1.77	William Wright, Jr., son of William Wright (Amherst County)
George G Wright		.24	George G. Wright, son of 1850 Jesse Wright of Nelson County, grandson of 1799 Benjamin Wright of Amherst County, and great grandson of 1767 Francis Wright of Amherst County
Jesse Wright		4.59	1850 Jesse Wright of Nelson County, son of 1799 Benjamin Wright of Amherst County and grandson of 1767 Frances Wright of Amherst County
Ellis Wright			1880 Ellis Wright of Amherst County, son of 1850 Jesse Wright of Nelson County, grandson of 1799 Benjamin Wright of Amherst County, and great grandson of 1767 Francis Wright of Amherst County
Austin Wright		3.06	1838 Augustine Wright of Nelson County, son of 1776 Augustine Wright of Amherst County

1827 PERSONAL PROPERTY TAX LIST

NELSON COUNTY, VIRGINIA

Appendix: Nelson County, Virginia, 1827 Personal Property Tax List:

District of Nelson Anderson:

Date of Receiving list _ Individuals	Persons names chargeable with Tax	Number of white males above 16 years	Blacks above 12 and under 16 years old	Blacks above 16 years old	Horses Mares Colts and Mules	Stud Horses and Jack Asses	Rate of covering p Season	Coaches Charriotts and Post Chaises	Other riding four wheeled Carriages	Riding Carriages with two wheels	Value of each Carriage
Feby 26	Benjamin Wright	2		3							
Feby 26	Andrew Wright	1			1						
Feby 26	Lucy Wright				2						
Feby 26	William Wright	1		2	3						
Mar 17	John Wright (BS)	1		1	1						
Mar 17	Austin Wright	1		7	2						
Mar 26	James Wright	1		6	3						
Mar 26	George G Wright	1			2						
Mar 26	Ellis Wright	1									
Mar 26	Shelton Wright	1									
Mar 26	William Wright Junr	1									

Appendix: Nelson County, Virginia, 1827 Personal Property Tax List:

District of Nelson Anderson:

Persons names chargeable with Tax [continued from prior page]	Tax on each Carriage D C	Sum Total of Taxes D C	Identification
Benjamin Wright		1.41	1861 Benjamin Wright of Nelson County, son of 1816 Andrew Wright of Nelson County and grandson of William Wright (Amherst County)
Andrew Wright		.12	Andrew Washington Wright, son of 1861 Benjamin Wright of Nelson County, grandson of 1816 Andrew Wright of Nelson County, and great grandson of William Wright (Amherst County)
Lucy Wright		.24	Lucy (Childress) Wright, wife of 1816 Andrew Wright of Nelson County, a son of William Wright (Amherst County)
William Wright		1.30	William Wright, Jr., son of William Wright (Amherst County)
John Wright		.59	John Wright, son of 1839 James Wright of Nelson County and grandson of William Wright (Amherst County)
Austin Wright		3.53	1838 Augustine Wright of Nelson County, son of 1776 Augustine Wright of Amherst County
James Wright		3.18	1839 James Wright of Nelson County, son of William Wright (Amherst County)
George G Wright		.24	George G. Wright, son of 1850 Jesse Wright of Nelson County, grandson of 1799 Benjamin Wright of Amherst County, and great grandson of 1767 Francis Wright of Amherst County
Ellis Wright			1880 Ellis Wright of Amherst County, son of 1850 Jesse Wright of Nelson County, grandson of 1799 Benjamin Wright of Amherst County, and great grandson of 1767 Francis Wright of Amherst County
Shelton Wright			1874 Shelton Wright of Nelson County, son of 1850 Jesse Wright of Nelson County, grandson of 1799 Benjamin Wright of Amherst County, and grandson of 1767 Francis Wright of Amherst County
William Wright Junr			1870 William Wright of Amherst County, son of 1850 Jesse Wright of Nelson County, grandson of 1799 Benjamin Wright of Amherst County, and great grandson of 1767 Francis Wright of Amherst County

Appendix: Nelson County, Virginia, 1827 Personal Property Tax List:

District of Nelson Anderson:

Date of Receiving list — Individuals	Persons names chargeable with Tax	Number of white males above 16 years	Blacks above 12 and under 16 years old	Blacks above 16 years old	Horses Mares Colts and Mules	Stud Horses and Jack Asses	Rate of covering p Season	Coaches Charriotts and Post Chaises	Other riding four wheeled Carriages	Riding Carriages with two wheels	Value of each Carriage
May 1	Jesse Wright	1	2	8	3						
May 26	Nelson Wright	1									

Appendix: Nelson County, Virginia, 1827 Personal Property Tax List:

District of Nelson Anderson:

Persons names chargeable with Tax [continued from prior page]	Tax on each Carriage D C	Sum Total of Taxes D C	Identification
Jesse Wright		5.06	1850 Jesse Wright of Nelson County, son of 1799 Benjamin Wright of Amherst County and grandson of 1767 Frances Wright of Amherst County
Nelson Wright			Nelson Wright, son of ____ Wright, grandson of 1839 James Wright of Nelson County, and great grandson of William Wright (Amherst County)

1828 PERSONAL PROPERTY TAX LIST

NELSON COUNTY, VIRGINIA

Appendix: Nelson County, Virginia, 1828 Personal Property Tax List:

District of Nelson Anderson:

Date of Receiving list __ Individuals	Persons names chargeable with Tax	blacks above 12 and under 16 years old	blacks above 16 years old	Horses Mares Colts and Mules	Stud Horses and Jack Asses	Rate of covering p Season	Coaches Charriots and Post Chaises	Other riding four wheeled Carriages	Riding Carriages with two wheels
Feby 25	William Wright	1		2	1				
Feby 25	George G Wright	1			1				
Feby 25	James Wright	1	2	4	5				
Feby 25	John Wright	1		2					
Feby 25	Benjamin Wright	2		1					
Feby 25	Lucy Wright			2					
Feby 25	Andrew Wright	1							
March 24	Shelton Wright	1			1				
March 24	Nelson Wright	1							
April 3	Jesse Wright	2	2	8	3				
April 3	Ellis Wright	1			1				

Appendix: Nelson County, Virginia, 1828 Personal Property Tax List:

District of Nelson Anderson:

Persons names chargeable with Tax [continued from prior page]	Tax on Carriages	Sum Total of Taxes	Identification
William Wright		1.06	William Wright, Jr., son of William Wright (Amherst County)
George G Wright		.12	George G. Wright, son of 1850 Jesse Wright of Nelson County, grandson of 1799 Benjamin Wright of Amherst County, and great grandson of 1767 Francis Wright of Amherst County
James Wright		3.42	1839 James Wright of Nelson County, son of William Wright (Amherst County)
John Wright		.94	John Wright, son of 1839 James Wright of Nelson County and grandson of William Wright (Amherst County)
Benjamin Wright		.47	1861 Benjamin Wright of Nelson County, son of 1816 Andrew Wright of Nelson County and grandson of William Wright (Amherst County)
Lucy Wright		.24	Lucy (Childress) Wright, wife of 1816 Andrew Wright of Nelson County, a son of William Wright (Amherst County)
Andrew Wright			Andrew Washington Wright, son of 1861 Benjamin Wright of Nelson County, grandson of 1816 Andrew Wright of Nelson County, and great grandson of William Wright (Amherst County)
Shelton Wright		.12	1874 Shelton Wright of Nelson County, son of 1850 Jesse Wright of Nelson County, grandson of 1799 Benjamin Wright of Amherst County, and grandson of 1767 Francis Wright of Amherst County
Nelson Wright			Nelson Wright, son of ____ Wright, grandson of 1839 James Wright of Nelson County, and great grandson of William Wright (Amherst County)
Jesse Wright		5.08	1850 Jesse Wright of Nelson County, son of 1799 Benjamin Wright of Amherst County and grandson of 1767 Frances Wright of Amherst County
Ellis Wright		.12	1880 Ellis Wright of Amherst County, son of 1850 Jesse Wright of Nelson County, grandson of 1799 Benjamin Wright of Amherst County, and great grandson of 1767 Francis Wright of Amherst County

Appendix: Nelson County, Virginia, 1828 Personal Property Tax List:

District of Nelson Anderson:

Date of Receiving list __ Individuals	Persons names chargeable with Tax	blacks above 12 and under 16 years old	blacks above 16 years old	Horses Mares Colts and Mules	Stud Horses and Jack Asses	Rate of covering p Season	Coaches Charriots and Post Chaises	Other riding four wheeled Carriages	Riding Carriages with two wheels
April 3	William Wright	1							
April 5	Wiatt Wright	1							
April 5	James Wright	1							
April 7	William B Wright	1							
April 23	Austin Wright	1		7	3				
__ 5	James Wright	1							
__ 5	Charles Wright	1							
__ 21	Wyatt Wright	1							

Appendix: Nelson County, Virginia, 1828 Personal Property Tax List:

District of Nelson Anderson:

Persons names chargeable with Tax [continued from prior page]	Tax on Carriages	Sum Total of Taxes	Identification
William Wright			1870 William Wright of Amherst County, son of 1850 Jesse Wright of Nelson County, grandson of 1799 Benjamin Wright of Amherst County, and great grandson of 1767 Francis Wright of Amherst County
Wiatt Wright			1889 Wyatt Wright of Gallia County, Ohio, son of Benjamin Wright, grandson of 1830 Moses Wright of Amherst County, great grandson of 1799 Benjamin Wright of Amherst County, and great great grandson of 1707 Francis Wright of Amherst County
James Wright			James Wright, son of Benjamin Wright, grandson of 1830 Moses Wright of Amherst County, great grandson of 1799 Benjamin Wright of Amherst County, and great great grandson of 1767 Francis Wright of Amherst County
William B Wright			
Austin Wright		3.65	1838 Augustine Wright of Nelson County, son of 1776 Augustine Wright of Amherst County
James Wright			James Wright, son of Benjamin Wright, grandson of 1830 Moses Wright of Amherst County, great grandson of 1799 Benjamin Wright of Amherst County, and great great grandson of 1767 Francis Wright of Amherst County
Charles Wright			1882 Charles H. Wright of Nelson County, son of Benjamin Wright, grandson of 1830 Moses Wright of Amherst County, great grandson of 1799 Benjamin Wright of Amherst County, and great great grandson of 1767 Francis Wright of Amherst County
Wyatt Wright			1889 Wyatt Wright of Gallia County, Ohio, son of Benjamin Wright, grandson of 1830 Moses Wright of Amherst County, great grandson of 1799 Benjamin Wright of Amherst County, and great great grandson of 1707 Francis Wright of Amherst County

1829 PERSONAL PROPERTY TAX LIST

NELSON COUNTY, VIRGINIA

Appendix: Nelson County, Virginia, 1829 Personal Property Tax List:

District of George Vughan Jr:

Date of Receiving list from Individuals	Persons names chargeable with Tax	Number of white males above 16 years old	Blacks above 12 and under 16 years old	Blacks above 16 years old	Horses mares Colts and mules	Stud horses and Jack Asses	Rate of covering per Season	Coaches Charriots and Post Chaises	Other riding four wheeled Carriages	Riding Carriages with two wheels	Value of each Carriage
Feby 14	Austin Wright	1		7	3						
Feby 23	Nelson Wright	1									
Feby 23	Ellis Wright	1			1						
Feby 23	Benjamin Wright	3	2	1							
Mar 12	Bennett Wright		1		1						
Mar 18	William B. Wright	1									
Mar 23	James Wright	1		7	5						
Mar 23	John Wright	1									
Mar 23	Shelton Wright	1		1							
Apl 4	James Wright	1									
Apl 4	William Wright (T.R.)	1			1						
Apl 4	Wyatt Wright	1									

Appendix: Nelson County, Virginia, 1829 Personal Property Tax List:

District of George Vaughan Jr:

Persons names chargeable with Tax [continued from prior page]	Tax on each Carriage D C	Sum Total of Taxes D C	Identification
Austin Wright		3.10	1838 Augustine Wright of Nelson County, son of 1776 Augustine Wright of Amherst County
Nelson Wright			Nelson Wright, son of ____ Wright, grandson of 1839 James Wright of Nelson County, and great grandson of William Wright (Amherst County)
Ellis Wright		.10	1880 Ellis Wright of Amherst County, son of 1850 Jesse Wright of Nelson County, grandson of 1799 Benjamin Wright of Amherst County, and great grandson of 1767 Francis Wright of Amherst County
Benjamin Wright		1.20	1861 Benjamin Wright of Nelson County, son of 1816 Andrew Wright of Nelson County and grandson of William Wright (Amherst County)
Bennett Wright		.40	
William B. Wright			
James Wright		3.30	1839 James Wright of Nelson County, son of William Wright (Amherst County)
John Wright			John Wright, son of 1839 James Wright of Nelson County and grandson of William Wright (Amherst County)
Shelton Wright		.10	1874 Shelton Wright of Nelson County, son of 1850 Jesse Wright of Nelson County, grandson of 1799 Benjamin Wright of Amherst County, and grandson of 1767 Francis Wright of Amherst County
James Wright			James Wright, son of Benjamin Wright, grandson of 1830 Moses Wright of Amherst County, great grandson of 1799 Benjamin Wright of Amherst County, and great great grandson of 1767 Francis Wright of Amherst County
William Wright (T.R.)		.10	1870 William Wright of Amherst County, son of 1850 Jesse Wright of Nelson County, grandson of 1799 Benjamin Wright of Amherst County, and great grandson of 1767 Francis Wright of Amherst County
Wyatt Wright			1889 Wyatt Wright of Gallia County, Ohio, son of Benjamin Wright, grandson of 1830 Moses Wright of Amherst County, great grandson of 1799 Benjamin Wright of Amherst County, and great great grandson of 1707 Francis Wright of Amherst County

Appendix: Nelson County, Virginia, 1829 Personal Property Tax List:

District of George Vughan Jr:

Date of Receiving list from Individuals	Persons names chargeable with Tax	Number of white males above 16 years old	Blacks above 12 and under 16 years old	Blacks above 16 years old	Horses mares Colts and mules	Stud horses and Jack Asses	Rate of covering per Season	Coaches Charriots and Post Chaises	Other riding four wheeled Carriages	Riding Carriages with two wheels	Value of each Carriage
Apl 6	Jesse Wright Senr	2	2	9	3						
Apl 6	Jesse Wright Jr.	1									
Apl 17	William Wright Senr	1		2	1						
Apl 17	Lucy Wright				2						

Appendix: Nelson County, Virginia, 1829 Personal Property Tax List:

District of George Vaughan Jr:

Persons names chargeable with Tax [continued from prior page]	Tax on each Carriage D C	Sum Total of Taxes D C	Identification
Jesse Wright Senr		4.70	1850 Jesse Wright of Nelson County, son of 1799 Benjamin Wright of Amherst County and grandson of 1767 Frances Wright of Amherst County
Jesse Wright Jr.			
William Wright Senr		.90	William Wright, Jr., son of William Wright (Amherst County)
Lucy Wright		.20	Lucy (Childress) Wright, wife of 1816 Andrew Wright of Nelson County, a son of William Wright (Amherst County)

1437(091908)

1830 PERSONAL PROPERTY TAX LIST

NELSON COUNTY, VIRGINIA

Appendix: Nelson County, Virginia, 1830 Personal Property Tax List:

District of George Vaughan Jr:

Date of receiving list from individuals	Persons names chargeable with Tax	Number of White males above 16 years old	Blacks above 12 and under 16 years old	Blacks above 16 years old	Horses Mares Colts and Mules	Stud Horses & Jack Asses	Rate of Covering pr Season	Coaches Chariots & Post Chaises	Other riding 4 wheeled carriages	Riding Carriages with 2 Wheels	Value of each Carriage
Feby 17	Austin Wright	1		9	4						
Feby 18	William Wright	1		1	1						
Feby 18	George G. Wright	1			1						
Feby 22	Nelson Wright	1									
Feby 22	John Wright	1									
Mar 10	Ellis Wright	1			1						
Mar 10	Wyatt Wright	1									
Mar 18	Bennett Wright	1		1							
Mar 22	Jesse Wright	2	2	7	4						
Mar 23	William Wright	1		2	1						
Mar 23	Est. Andrew Wright				2						

Appendix: Nelson County, Virginia, 1830 Personal Property Tax List:

District of George Vaughan Jr:

Persons names chargeable with Tax [continued from prior page]	Tax on each Carriage D C	Sum total of Taxes D C	Identification
Austin Wright		3.47	1838 Augustine Wright of Nelson County, son of 1776 Augustine Wright of Amherst County
William Wright		.43	Probably 1870 William Wright of Amherst County, son of 1850 Jesse Wright of Nelson County, grandson of 1799 Benjamin Wright of Amherst County, and great grandson of 1767 Francis Wright of Amherst County
George G. Wright		.08	George G. Wright, son of 1850 Jesse Wright of Nelson County, grandson of 1799 Benjamin Wright of Amherst County, and great grandson of 1767 Francis Wright of Amherst County
Nelson Wright			Nelson Wright, son of ____ Wright, grandson of 1839 James Wright of Nelson County, and great grandson of William Wright (Amherst County)
John Wright			John Wright, son of 1839 James Wright of Nelson County and grandson of William Wright (Amherst County)
Ellis Wright		.08	1880 Ellis Wright of Amherst County, son of 1850 Jesse Wright of Nelson County, grandson of 1799 Benjamin Wright of Amherst County, and great grandson of 1767 Francis Wright of Amherst County
Wyatt Wright			1889 Wyatt Wright of Gallia County, Ohio, son of Benjamin Wright, grandson of 1830 Moses Wright of Amherst County, great grandson of 1799 Benjamin Wright of Amherst County, and great great grandson of 1707 Francis Wright of Amherst County
Bennett Wright		.35	
Jesse Wright		3.47	1850 Jesse Wright of Nelson County, son of 1799 Benjamin Wright of Amherst County and grandson of 1767 Frances Wright of Amherst County
William Wright		.78	William Wright, Jr., son of William Wright (Amherst County)
Est. Andrew Wright		.16	Estate of 1816 Andrew Wright of Nelson County, son of William Wright (Amherst County)

1437(091908)

Appendix: Nelson County, Virginia, 1830 Personal Property Tax List:

District of George Vaughan Jr:

Date of receiving list from individuals	Persons names chargeable with Tax	Number of White males above 16 years old	Blacks above 12 and under 16 years old	Blacks above 16 years old	Horses Mares Colts and Mules	Stud Horses & Jack Asses	Rate of Covering pr Season	Coaches Chariots & Post Chaises	Other riding 4 wheeled carriages	Riding Carriages with 2 Wheels	Value of each Carriage
Mar 29	Benjamin Wright	1									
Apl 3	James Wright	1	3	4	4	1	5				

Appendix: Nelson County, Virginia, 1830 Personal Property Tax List:

District of George Vaughan Jr:

Persons names chargeable with Tax [continued from prior page]	Tax on each Carriage D C	Sum total of Taxes D C	Identification
Benjamin Wright			1861 Benjamin Wright of Nelson County, son of 1816 Andrew Wright of Nelson County and grandson of William Wright (Amherst County)
James Wright		12.77	1839 James Wright of Nelson County, son of William Wright (Amherst County)

Appendix: Nelson County, Virginia, 1830 Personal Property Tax List:

District of George Vaughan Jr:

Date of receiving list from individuals	Persons names chargeable with Tax	Number of White males above 16 years old	Blacks above 12 and under 16 years old	Blacks above 16 years old	Horses Mares Colts and Mules	Stud Horses & Jack Asses	Rate of Covering pr Season	Coaches Chariots & Post Chaises	Other riding 4 wheeled carriages	Riding Carriages with 2 Wheels	Value of each Carriage
Apl 3	John B. Wright	1									
Apl 26	William B. Wright	1									

Appendix: Nelson County, Virginia, 1830 Personal Property Tax List:

District of George Vaughan Jr:

Persons names chargeable with Tax [continued from prior page]	Tax on each Carriage D C	Sum total of Taxes D C	Identification
John B. Wright			John B. Wright, son of 1861 Benjamin Wright of Nelson County, grandson of 1816 Andrew Wright of Nelson County, and great grandson of William Wright (Amherst County)
William B. Wright			

1831 PERSONAL PROPERTY TAX LIST

NELSON COUNTY, VIRGINIA

Appendix: Nelson County, Virginia, 1831 Personal Property Tax List:

District of Nathan C Anderson:

Date of receiving list from Individuals	Persons Names Chargeable With Tax	Number of white males above 16 years of age	Blacks above 12 and under 16 years of age	Blacks above 16 years of age	Horses Mares Colts & Mules	Stud Horses and Jack Asses	Rates of Covering pr Season	Coaches Chariots and post Chaises	Other riding four Wheel Carriages	Riding Carriages with Two Wheels	Value of each Carriage
Feby 1	Bennet Wright	1		1							
Feby 23	John B Wright	1									
Feby 23	Wm Wright	1		2							
Feby 25	Benjamin Wright	1			1						
Feby 25	Andrew W Wright	1									
Feby 28	Nelson Wright	1									
Feby 28	John Wright	1									
Feby 28	George G Wright	1			1						
March 15	Austin Wright	1		10	3						
March 15	Wm B Wright	1									
March 28	James Wright	1	3	5	7						
March 28	John Wright	1									

Appendix: Nelson County, Virginia, 1831 Personal Property Tax List:

District of George Vaughan Jr:

Persons Names Chargeable with Tax [continued from prior page]	Tax on each Carriage D C	Sum Total of Taxes D C	Identification
Bennet Wright		.25	
John B Wright			John B. Wright, son of 1861 Benjamin Wright of Nelson County, grandson of 1816 Andrew Wright of Nelson County, and great grandson of William Wright (Amherst County)
Wm Wright		.50	William Wright, Jr., son of William Wright (Amherst County)
Benjamin Wright		.06	1861 Benjamin Wright of Nelson County, son of 1816 Andrew Wright of Nelson County and grandson of William Wright (Amherst County)
Andrew W Wright			Andrew Washington Wright, son of 1861 Benjamin Wright of Nelson County, grandson of 1816 Andrew Wright of Nelson County, and great grandson of William Wright (Amherst County)
Nelson Wright			Nelson Wright, son of ____ Wright, grandson of 1839 James Wright of Nelson County, and great grandson of William Wright (Amherst County)
John Wright			John Wright, son of 1839 James Wright of Nelson County and grandson of William Wright (Amherst County)
George G Wright		.06	George G. Wright, son of 1850 Jesse Wright of Nelson County, grandson of 1799 Benjamin Wright of Amherst County, and great grandson of 1767 Francis Wright of Amherst County
Austin Wright		2.68	1838 Augustine Wright of Nelson County, son of 1776 Augustine Wright of Amherst County
Wm B Wright			
James Wright		2.42	1839 James Wright of Nelson County, son of William Wright (Amherst County)
John Wright			Probably John Wright, son of 1839 James Wright of Nelson County and grandson of William Wright (Amherst County) [possible duplicate listing]

Appendix: Nelson County, Virginia, 1831 Personal Property Tax List:

District of Nathan C Anderson:

Date of receiving list from Individuals	Persons Names Chargeable With Tax	Number of white males above 16 years of age	Blacks above 12 and under 16 years of age	Blacks above 16 years of age	Horses Mares Colts & Mules	Stud Horses and Jack Asses	Rates of Covering pr Season	Coaches Chariots and post Chaises	Other riding four Wheel Carriages	Riding Carriages with Two Wheels	Value of each Carriage
Apl. 12	Jesse Wright	2	2	7	5						
May 12	Ellis Wright	1			2						
Apl 12	Shelton Wright	1		1							
Apl 12	Wyatt Wright	1									
Apl 28	Lucy Wright				2						

Appendix: Nelson County, Virginia, 1831 Personal Property Tax List:

District of George Vaughan Jr:

Persons Names Chargeable with Tax [continued from prior page]	Tax on each Carriage D C	Sum Total of Taxes D C	Identification
Jesse Wright		2.55	1850 Jesse Wright of Nelson County, son of 1799 Benjamin Wright of Amherst County and grandson of 1767 Frances Wright of Amherst County
Ellis Wright		.12	1880 Ellis Wright of Amherst County, son of 1850 Jesse Wright of Nelson County, grandson of 1799 Benjamin Wright of Amherst County, and great grandson of 1767 Francis Wright of Amherst County
Shelton Wright		.25	1874 Shelton Wright of Nelson County, son of 1850 Jesse Wright of Nelson County, grandson of 1799 Benjamin Wright of Amherst County, and grandson of 1767 Francis Wright of Amherst County
Wyatt Wright			1889 Wyatt Wright of Gallia County, Ohio, son of Benjamin Wright, grandson of 1830 Moses Wright of Amherst County, great grandson of 1799 Benjamin Wright of Amherst County, and great great grandson of 1707 Francis Wright of Amherst County
Lucy Wright		.12	Lucy (Childress) Wright, wife of 1816 Andrew Wright of Nelson County, a son of William Wright (Amherst County)

1832 PERSONAL PROPERTY TAX LIST

NELSON COUNTY, VIRGINIA

Appendix: Nelson County, Virginia, 1832 Personal Property Tax List:

District of Nathan C Anderson:

Date of Receiving lists of Individuals		Number of White Males above 16 years of age	Blacks above 12 & under 16 years of age	Blacks above 16 years of age	Horses Mares Colts & Mules	Stud Horses & Jack Asses	Rates of Covering pr Season	Coaches Chariots & Post Chaises	Other Riding four wheel Carriages	Riding Carriages with two Wheels	Value of each Carriage
Feby 25	Andrew W Wright	1									
Feby 25	George G. Wright	1		1	1						
Feby 25	Austin Wright	1	2	9	3						
March 26	John R. Wright	1		1							
March 27	Benjamin Wright	1		1	1						
March 27	John Wright	1									
March 27	James Wright	1	2	6	6	1	6				
April 6	Jesse Wright	1	1	8	4						
April 6	Ellis Wright	1			3						
April 6	Shelton Wright	1									
Apl 13	Wm B. Wright	1									

Appendix: Nelson County, Virginia, 1832 Personal Property Tax List:

District of Nathan C. Anderson:

[continued from prior page]	Tax on each Carriage D C	Sum Total of Taxes D C	Identification
Andrew W Wright			Andrew Washington Wright, son of 1861 Benjamin Wright of Nelson County, grandson of 1816 Andrew Wright of Nelson County, and great grandson of William Wright (Amherst County)
George G. Wright		.31	George G. Wright, son of 1850 Jesse Wright of Nelson County, grandson of 1799 Benjamin Wright of Amherst County, and great grandson of 1767 Francis Wright of Amherst County
Austin Wright		2.93	1838 Augustine Wright of Nelson County, son of 1776 Augustine Wright of Amherst County
John R. Wright		.06	John B. Wright, son of 1861 Benjamin Wright of Nelson County, grandson of 1816 Andrew Wright of Nelson County, and great grandson of William Wright (Amherst County)
Benjamin Wright		.31	1861 Benjamin Wright of Nelson County, son of 1816 Andrew Wright of Nelson County and grandson of William Wright (Amherst County)
John Wright			John Wright, son of 1839 James Wright of Nelson County and grandson of William Wright (Amherst County)
James Wright		14.36	1839 James Wright of Nelson County, son of William Wright (Amherst County)
Jesse Wright		2.49	1850 Jesse Wright of Nelson County, son of 1799 Benjamin Wright of Amherst County and grandson of 1767 Frances Wright of Amherst County
Ellis Wright		.18	1880 Ellis Wright of Amherst County, son of 1850 Jesse Wright of Nelson County, grandson of 1799 Benjamin Wright of Amherst County, and great grandson of 1767 Francis Wright of Amherst County
Shelton Wright			1874 Shelton Wright of Nelson County, son of 1850 Jesse Wright of Nelson County, grandson of 1799 Benjamin Wright of Amherst County, and grandson of 1767 Francis Wright of Amherst County
Wm B. Wright			

Appendix: Nelson County, Virginia, 1832 Personal Property Tax List:

District of Nathan C Anderson:

Date of Receiving lists of Individuals		Number of White Males above 16 years of age	Blacks above 12 & under 16 years of age	Blacks above 16 years of age	Horses Mares Colts & Mules	Stud Horses & Jack Asses	Rates of Covering pr Season	Coaches Chariots & Post Chaises	Other Riding four wheel Carriages	Riding Carriages with two Wheels	Value of each Carriage
gApl 23	Nelson Wright	1									
Apl 23	Bennet Wright	1		1							
May 4	Wm Wright	1		2							
May 4	Lucy Wright				1						

Appendix: Nelson County, Virginia, 1832 Personal Property Tax List:

District of Nathan C. Anderson:

[continued from prior page]	Tax on each Carriage D C	Sum Total of Taxes D C	Identification
Nelson Wright			Nelson Wright, son of ____ Wright, grandson of 1839 James Wright of Nelson County, and great grandson of William Wright (Amherst County)
Bennet Wright		.25	
Wm Wright		.50	William Wright, Jr., son of William Wright (Amherst County)
Lucy Wright		.06	Lucy (Childress) Wright, wife of 1816 Andrew Wright of Nelson County, a son of William Wright (Amherst County)

1833 PERSONAL PROPERTY TAX LIST

NELSON COUNTY, VIRGINIA

Appendix: Nelson County, Virginia, 1833 Personal Property Tax List:

District of Nathan C Anderson:

	Persons names Chargeable With Tax	of White Males above 16 Years of age	above 12 & under 16 Years of age	above 16 Years of age	Mares Colts & Mules	Stud Horses & Jack Asses	Rates of Covering pr Season	Coaches Chariots and Post Chaises	Other riding four wheel Carriages	Riding Carriages with Two Wheels	Value of each Carriage
March 13	Austin Wright	1	1	9	3						
March 25	John B Wright	1									
March 25	Benjamin Wright	1			1						
March 25	Wm Wright	1		1							
March 25	Nelson Wright	1									
March 25	Andrew W Wright	1			1						
April 6	Wm Wright	1			1						
April 11	James Wright	2	2	7	7						
April 11	Jesse Wright	1	1	8	3						
April 11	George G Wright	1			1						
April 11	Daniel L Wright	1									
	Wm Wright	1									

Appendix: Nelson County, Virginia, 1833 Personal Property Tax List:

District of Nathan C. Anderson:

Persons Names Chargeable With Tax [continued from prior page]	Tax on each Carriage D C	Sum Total of Taxes D C	Identification
Austin Wright		2.68	1838 Augustine Wright of Nelson County, son of 1776 Augustine Wright of Amherst County
John B Wright			John B. Wright, son of 1861 Benjamin Wright of Nelson County, grandson of 1816 Andrew Wright of Nelson County, and great grandson of William Wright (Amherst County)
Benjamin Wright		.06	1861 Benjamin Wright of Nelson County, son of 1816 Andrew Wright of Nelson County and grandson of William Wright (Amherst County)
Wm Wright		.25	
Nelson Wright			
Andrew W Wright		.06	Andrew Washington Wright, son of 1861 Benjamin Wright of Nelson County, grandson of 1816 Andrew Wright of Nelson County, and great grandson of William Wright (Amherst County)
Wm Wright		.06	
James Wright		2.67	
Jesse Wright		2.43	1850 Jesse Wright of Nelson County, son of 1799 Benjamin Wright of Amherst County and grandson of 1767 Frances Wright of Amherst County
George G Wright		.06	George G. Wright, son of 1850 Jesse Wright of Nelson County, grandson of 1799 Benjamin Wright of Amherst County, and great grandson of 1767 Francis Wright of Amherst County
Daniel L Wright			1882 Daniel L. Wright of Amherst County, son of 1850 Jesse Wright of Nelson County, grandson of 1799 Benjamin Wright of Amherst County, and great grandson of 1767 Francis Wright of Amherst County
Wm Wright			

1834 PERSONAL PROPERTY TAX LIST

NELSON COUNTY, VIRGINIA

Appendix: Nelson County, Virginia, 1834 Personal Property Tax List:

District of Nathan C Anderson:

	Persons names Chargeable With Tax	Number of White Males above 16 Years of age	Blacks above 12 & under 16 Years of age	Blacks above 16 Years of age	Horses Mares Colts & Mules	Stud Horses & Jack Asses	Rates of Covering pr Season	Carriage Wheels			Value of each Carriage
								Coaches Chariots and Post Chaises	Other Riding four Wheel Carriages	Riding Carriages with Two Wheels	
Feby 22	John B Wright	1		1							
Feby 27	Wm R Wright	1		2	3						
March 11	John Wright	1									
March 11	Andrew W Wright	1			1						
March 25	Benjamin Wright	1		1	2						
March 25	Wm Wright Snr	1			1						
April 4	Nelson Wright	1									
April 4	Jesse Wright	1	1	6	5						
April 4	George G Wright	1	1	2	1						
April 4	Ellis Wright	1			2						
April 4	Shelton Wright	1									

Appendix: Nelson County, Virginia, 1834 Personal Property Tax List:

District of Nathan C. Anderson:

Persons names Chargeable With Tax [continued from prior page]	Tax on each Carriage D C	Sum Total of Taxes D C	Identification
John B Wright		.25	John B. Wright, son of 1861 Benjamin Wright of Nelson County, grandson of 1816 Andrew Wright of Nelson County, and great grandson of William Wright (Amherst County)
Wm R Wright		.68	1871 William R. Wright of Buckingham County, son of 1842 Thomas Wright of Buckingham County
John Wright			
Andrew W Wright		.06	Andrew Washington Wright, son of 1861 Benjamin Wright of Nelson County, grandson of 1816 Andrew Wright of Nelson County, and great grandson of William Wright (Amherst County)
Benjamin Wright		.37	1861 Benjamin Wright of Nelson County, son of 1816 Andrew Wright of Nelson County and grandson of William Wright (Amherst County)
Wm Wright Snr		.06	William Wright, Jr., son of William Wright (Amherst County)
Nelson Wright			Nelson Wright, son of ____ Wright, grandson of 1839 James Wright of Nelson County, and great grandson of William Wright (Amherst County)
Jesse Wright		2.05	1850 Jesse Wright of Nelson County, son of 1799 Benjamin Wright of Amherst County and grandson of 1767 Frances Wright of Amherst County
George G Wright		.81	George G. Wright, son of 1850 Jesse Wright of Nelson County, grandson of 1799 Benjamin Wright of Amherst County, and great grandson of 1767 Francis Wright of Amherst County
Ellis Wright		.12	1880 Ellis Wright of Amherst County, son of 1850 Jesse Wright of Nelson County, grandson of 1799 Benjamin Wright of Amherst County, and great grandson of 1767 Francis Wright of Amherst County
Shelton Wright			1874 Shelton Wright of Nelson County, son of 1850 Jesse Wright of Nelson County, grandson of 1799 Benjamin Wright of Amherst County, and grandson of 1767 Francis Wright of Amherst County

Appendix: Nelson County, Virginia, 1834 Personal Property Tax List:

District of Nathan C Anderson:

	Persons names Chargeable With Tax	Number of White Males above 16 Years of age	Blacks above 12 & under 16 Years of age	Blacks above 16 Years of age	Horses Mares Colts & Mules	Stud Horses & Jack Asses	Rates of Covering pr Season	Coaches Chariots and Post Chaises	Other Riding four Wheel Carriages	Riding Carriages with Two Wheels	Value of each Carriage
April 4	Wm Wright	1									
April 28	Austin Wright	1	1	8	3						
April 28	James Wright	1	3	6	5						
April 28	John Wright	1									

Appendix: Nelson County, Virginia, 1834 Personal Property Tax List:

District of Nathan C. Anderson:

Persons names Chargeable With Tax [continued from prior page]	Tax on each Carriage D C	Sum Total of Taxes D C	Identification
Wm Wright			
Austin Wright		2.43	1838 Augustine Wright of Nelson County, son of 1776 Augustine Wright of Amherst County
James Wright		2.55	1839 James Wright of Nelson County, son of William Wright (Amherst County)
John Wright			John Wright, son of 1839 James Wright of Nelson County and grandson of William Wright (Amherst County)

1437(091908)

1835 PERSONAL PROPERTY TAX LIST

NELSON COUNTY, VIRGINIA

Appendix: Nelson County, Virginia, 1835 Personal Property Tax List:

District of Nathan C Anderson:

Date of receiving lists of Individuals	Persons Names Chargeable With Tax	Number of White Males above 16 Years	Blacks above 12 & under 16 Years of age	Blacks above 16 Years of age	Horses Mares Colts & Mules	Stud Horses & Jack Asses	Rates of Covering pr Season	Carriage Wheels Coaches Chariots and Post Chaises	Other riding four Wheel Carriages	Riding Carriages with Two Wheels	Value of each Carriage
Feby 6	Wm B Wright	1									
March 22	Benjamin Wright	2	1	1	1						
March 22	John B Wright	1		1							
March 22	Andrew W Wright	1			2						
Apl 3	Wm R. Wright	1		2	3						
Apl 6	George G Wright	1	3	8	5						
Apl 6	Jesse Wright	1									
Apl 6	Wm Wright	1									
Apl 10	Nelson Wright	1									

Appendix: Nelson County, Virginia, 1835 Personal Property Tax List:

District of Nathan C. Anderson:

Persons Names Chargeable With Tax [continued from prior page]	Tax on each Carriage D C	Sum Total of Taxes D C	Identification
Wm B Wright			
Benjamin Wright		.66	1861 Benjamin Wright of Nelson County, son of 1816 Andrew Wright of Nelson County and grandson of William Wright (Amherst County)
John B Wright		.25	John B. Wright, son of 1861 Benjamin Wright of Nelson County, grandson of 1816 Andrew Wright of Nelson County, and great grandson of William Wright (Amherst County)
Andrew W Wright		.12	Andrew Washington Wright, son of 1861 Benjamin Wright of Nelson County, grandson of 1816 Andrew Wright of Nelson County, and great grandson of William Wright (Amherst County)
Wm R. Wright		.68	1871 William R. Wright of Buckingham County, son of 1842 Thomas Wright of Buckingham County
George G Wright		3.05	George G. Wright, son of 1850 Jesse Wright of Nelson County, grandson of 1799 Benjamin Wright of Amherst County, and great grandson of 1767 Francis Wright of Amherst County
Jesse Wright			1850 Jesse Wright of Nelson County, son of 1799 Benjamin Wright of Amherst County and grandson of 1767 Frances Wright of Amherst County
Wm Wright			
Nelson Wright			Nelson Wright, son of ____ Wright, grandson of 1839 James Wright of Nelson County, and great grandson of William Wright (Amherst County)

1437(091908)

1836 PERSONAL PROPERTY TAX LIST

NELSON COUNTY, VIRGINIA

Appendix: Nelson County, Virginia, 1836 Personal Property Tax List:

District of Nathan C Anderson:

Date of receiving list of Individuals		Number of White Males above 16 years of age	Blacks above 12 years of age and under 16	Blacks above 16 Years of age	Horses Mares Colts & Mules	Stud Horses & Jack Asses	Rates of Covering pr Season	Carriage Wheels			Value of each Carriage
								Coaches Chariots and Post Chaises	Other riding four Wheel Carriages	Riding Carriages with Two Wheels	
Feby 22	Benjamin Wright	1		1							
Feby 22	Andrew W Wright	1			3						
Feby 22	Austin Wright	1	1	10	3						
March 18	Wm B Wright	1									
March 28	James Wright	1	1	9	5						
March 28	John Wright	1									
March 28	Wm R Wright	1		3	3						
March 28	Nelson Wright	1									
Apl 4	Wm Wright	1			1						
Apl 8	John B Wright	1									
May 10	Ellis Wright	1			1						
May 10	George G Wright	1	4	8	5						

Appendix: Nelson County, Virginia, 1836 Personal Property Tax List:

District of Nathan C. Anderson:

[continued from prior page]	Tax on each Carriage D C	Sum Total of Taxes D C	Identification
Benjamin Wright		.25	1861 Benjamin Wright of Nelson County, son of 1816 Andrew Wright of Nelson County and grandson of William Wright (Amherst County)
Andrew W Wright		.18	Andrew Washington Wright, son of 1861 Benjamin Wright of Nelson County, grandson of 1816 Andrew Wright of Nelson County, and great grandson of William Wright (Amherst County)
Austin Wright		2.93	1838 Augustine Wright of Nelson County, son of 1776 Augustine Wright of Amherst County
Wm B Wright			
James Wright		2.80	1839 James Wright of Nelson County, son of William Wright (Amherst County)
John Wright			John Wright, son of 1839 James Wright of Nelson County and grandson of William Wright (Amherst County)
Wm R Wright		.93	1871 William R. Wright of Buckingham County, son of 1842 Thomas Wright of Buckingham County
Nelson Wright			Nelson Wright, son of ____ Wright, grandson of 1839 James Wright of Nelson County, and great grandson of William Wright (Amherst County)
Wm Wright		.06	
John B Wright			John B. Wright, son of 1861 Benjamin Wright of Nelson County, grandson of 1816 Andrew Wright of Nelson County, and great grandson of William Wright (Amherst County)
Ellis Wright		.06	1880 Ellis Wright of Amherst County, son of 1850 Jesse Wright of Nelson County, grandson of 1799 Benjamin Wright of Amherst County, and great grandson of 1767 Francis Wright of Amherst County
George G Wright		3.30	George G. Wright, son of 1850 Jesse Wright of Nelson County, grandson of 1799 Benjamin Wright of Amherst County, and great grandson of 1767 Francis Wright of Amherst County

Appendix: Nelson County, Virginia, 1836 Personal Property Tax List:

District of Nathan C Anderson:

Date of receiving list of Individuals		Number of White Males above 16 years of age	Blacks above 12 years of age and under 16	Blacks above 16 Years of age	Horses Mares Colts & Mules	Stud Horses & Jack Asses	Rates of Covering pr Season	Carriage Wheels			Value of each Carriage
								Coaches Chariots and Post Chaises	Other riding four Wheel Carriages	Riding Carriages with Two Wheels	
May 10	Jesse Wright	1									
May 10	Daniel L Wright	1			1						

Appendix: Nelson County, Virginia, 1836 Personal Property Tax List:

District of Nathan C. Anderson:

[continued from prior page]	Tax on each Carriage <u>D C</u>	Sum Total of Taxes <u>D C</u>	Identification
Jesse Wright			1850 Jesse Wright of Nelson County, son of 1799 Benjamin Wright of Amherst County and grandson of 1767 Frances Wright of Amherst County
Daniel L Wright		.06	1882 Daniel L. Wright of Amherst County, son of 1850 Jesse Wright of Nelson County, grandson of 1799 Benjamin Wright of Amherst County, and great grandson of 1767 Francis Wright of Amherst County

1437(091908)

137.

1837 PERSONAL PROPERTY TAX LIST

NELSON COUNTY, VIRGINIA

Appendix: Nelson County, Virginia, 1837 Personal Property Tax List:

District of Nathan C Anderson:

Date of receiving list of Individuals	Persons Names Chargeable With Tax	Number of White Males above 16 years of age	Blacks above 12 and under 16 years of age	Blacks above 16 Years of age	Horses Mares Colts and Mules	Stud Horses and Jack Asses	Rates of Covering pr Season	Coaches Chariots and Post Chaises	Other Riding four Wheel Carriages	Riding Carriages with Two Wheels	Value of each Carriage
Feby 4	Danl L Wright	1			1						
Feby 4	Wm R Wright	1		1	3						
Feby 4	John W Wright	1		1	1						
Feby 4	G G Wright	2	3	6	5						
Feby 10	Austin Wright	1	1	10	3						
Feby 10	Nelson Wright	1									
Feby 10	Benjamin Wright	2									
March 5	John Wright	1	1	1							
March 5	Andrew W Wright	1			3						
Apl 12	Shelton Wright	1									
Apl 12	Wm Wright	1			1						
Apl 28	James Wright	2		7	7						

1437(091908)

Appendix: Nelson County, Virginia, 1837 Personal Property Tax List:

District of Nathan C. Anderson:

Persons Names Chargeable With Taxes [continued from prior page]	Tax on each Carriage	Sum Total of Taxes	Identification
Danl L Wright		.06	1882 Daniel L. Wright of Amherst County, son of 1850 Jesse Wright of Nelson County, grandson of 1799 Benjamin Wright of Amherst County, and great grandson of 1767 Francis Wright of Amherst County
Wm R Wright		.43	1871 William R. Wright of Buckingham County, son of 1842 Thomas Wright of Buckingham County
John W Wright		.31	
G G Wright		2.55	George G. Wright, son of 1850 Jesse Wright of Nelson County, grandson of 1799 Benjamin Wright of Amherst County, and great grandson of 1767 Francis Wright of Amherst County
Austin Wright		2.93	1838 Augustine Wright of Nelson County, son of 1776 Augustine Wright of Amherst County
Nelson Wright			Nelson Wright, son of ____ Wright, grandson of 1839 James Wright of Nelson County, and great grandson of William Wright (Amherst County)
Benjamin Wright			1861 Benjamin Wright of Nelson County, son of 1816 Andrew Wright of Nelson County and grandson of William Wright (Amherst County)
John Wright		.50	
Andrew W Wright		.18	Andrew Washington Wright, son of 1861 Benjamin Wright of Nelson County, grandson of 1816 Andrew Wright of Nelson County, and great grandson of William Wright (Amherst County)
Shelton Wright			1874 Shelton Wright of Nelson County, son of 1850 Jesse Wright of Nelson County, grandson of 1799 Benjamin Wright of Amherst County, and grandson of 1767 Francis Wright of Amherst County
Wm Wright		.06	
James Wright		2.17	1839 James Wright of Nelson County, son of William Wright (Amherst County)

1838 PERSONAL PROPERTY TAX LIST

NELSON COUNTY, VIRGINIA

Appendix: Nelson County, Virginia, 1838 Personal Property Tax List:

District of Nathan C Anderson:

Date of receiving list of Property		Number of White Males above 16 Years of age	Blacks above 12 and under 16 Years of age	Blacks above 16 Years of age	Horses Mares Colts and Mules	Stud Horses and Jack Asses	Rates of Covering pr Season	Coaches Chariots and Post Chaises	Other Riding four Wheel Carriages	Riding Carriages with Two Wheels	Value of each Carriage D C
Feby 26	Wm R Wright	1		1	1						
Feby 26	Wm B Wright	1									
Feby 26	Daniel L Wright	1			1						
Feby 26	Charles Wright	1			2						
Feby 26	Henry Wright	1									
Feby 26	Robert M Wright	1			2						
March 1	John B Wright	1	1	1							
March 1	Benjamin Wright	3									
March 1	Andrew W Wright	1			1						
March 26	James Wright	2	2	7	6						
March 26	George G Wright	2	2	7	4						

Appendix: Nelson County, Virginia, 1838 Personal Property Tax List:

District of Nathan C. Anderson:

[continued from prior page]	Tax on each Carriage D C	Sum Total of Taxes D C	Identification
Wm R Wright		.38	1871 William R. Wright of Buckingham County, son of 1842 Thomas Wright of Buckingham County
Wm B Wright			
Daniel L Wright		.08	1882 Daniel L. Wright of Amherst County, son of 1850 Jesse Wright of Nelson County, grandson of 1799 Benjamin Wright of Amherst County, and great grandson of 1767 Francis Wright of Amherst County
Charles Wright		.16	1882 Charles H. Wright of Nelson County, son of Benjamin Wright, grandson of 1830 Moses Wright of Amherst County, great grandson of 1799 Benjamin Wright of Amherst County, and great great grandson of 1767 Francis Wright of Amherst County
Henry Wright			
Robert M Wright		.16	1855 Robert M. Wright of Nelson County, son of Mary Wright, grandson of 1816 Andrew Wright of Nelson County, and great grandson of William Wright (Amherst County)
John B Wright		.60	John B. Wright, son of 1861 Benjamin Wright of Nelson County, grandson of 1816 Andrew Wright of Nelson County, and great grandson of William Wright (Amherst County)
Benjamin Wright			1861 Benjamin Wright of Nelson County, son of 1816 Andrew Wright of Nelson County and grandson of William Wright (Amherst County)
Andrew W Wright		.08	Andrew Washington Wright, son of 1861 Benjamin Wright of Nelson County, grandson of 1816 Andrew Wright of Nelson County, and great grandson of William Wright (Amherst County)
James Wright		3.18	1839 James Wright of Nelson County, son of William Wright (Amherst County)
George G Wright		3.02	George G. Wright, son of 1850 Jesse Wright of Nelson County, grandson of 1799 Benjamin Wright of Amherst County, and great grandson of 1767 Francis Wright of Amherst County

Appendix: Nelson County, Virginia, 1838 Personal Property Tax List:

District of Nathan C Anderson:

Date of receiving list of Property		Number of White Males above 16 Years of age	Blacks above 12 and under 16 Years of age	Blacks above 16 Years of age	Horses Mares Colts and Mules	Stud Horses and Jack Asses	Rates of Covering pr Season	Coaches Chariots and Post Chaises	Other Riding four Wheel Carriages	Riding Carriages with Two Wheels	Value of each Carriage D C
March 26	Austin Wright	1	1	9	3						
Apl 16	Nelson Wright	1									
Apl 20	Wm Wright	1			1						

Appendix: Nelson County, Virginia, 1838 Personal Property Tax List:

District of Nathan C. Anderson:

[continued from prior page]	Tax on each Carriage D C	Sum Total of Taxes D C	Identification
Austin Wright		3.24	1838 Augustine Wright of Nelson County, son of 1776 Augustine Wright of Amherst County
Nelson Wright			Nelson Wright, son of ____ Wright, grandson of 1839 James Wright of Nelson County, and great grandson of William Wright (Amherst County)
Wm Wright		.08	

1839 PERSONAL PROPERTY TAX LIST

NELSON COUNTY, VIRGINIA

Appendix: Nelson County, Virginia, 1839 Personal Property Tax List:

District of Nathan C Anderson:

Date of receiving list of Individuals		Number of White Males above 16 Years of age	Blacks above 12 and under 16 Years of age	Blacks above 16 Years of age	Horses Colts Mares Mules Jacks and	Stud Horses and Jack Asses	Rates of Covering pr Season	Coaches Chariots and Post Chaises	Other Riding four Wheel Carriages	Riding Carriages with Two Wheels	Value of each Carriage D C
March 3	Chas Wright	1			1						
March 25	John B Wright	1	1		1						
March 25	Andrew W Wright	1			1						
March 25	Shelton Wright	1	1	4	3						
March 25	Benjamin Wright	3			1						
Apl 22	James Wright	2	2	7	7						
Apl 22	Danl L Wright	1	1	2	2						
Apl 22	Jesse Wright	1		3	2						
Apl 22	Wm Wright	1			1						
March 11	Wm R Wright	1			1						
March 11	Nelson Wright	1									

1437(091908)

Appendix: Nelson County, Virginia, 1839 Personal Property Tax List:

District of Nathan C. Anderson:

[continued from prior page]	Tax on each Carriage D C	Sum Total of Taxes D C	Identification
Chas Wright		.08	1882 Charles H. Wright of Nelson County, son of Benjamin Wright, grandson of 1830 Moses Wright of Amherst County, great grandson of 1799 Benjamin Wright of Amherst County, and great great grandson of 1767 Francis Wright of Amherst County
John B Wright		.38	John B. Wright, son of 1861 Benjamin Wright of Nelson County, grandson of 1816 Andrew Wright of Nelson County, and great grandson of William Wright (Amherst County)
Andrew W Wright		.08	Andrew Washington Wright, son of 1861 Benjamin Wright of Nelson County, grandson of 1816 Andrew Wright of Nelson County, and great grandson of William Wright (Amherst County)
Shelton Wright		1.74	1874 Shelton Wright of Nelson County, son of 1850 Jesse Wright of Nelson County, grandson of 1799 Benjamin Wright of Amherst County, and grandson of 1767 Francis Wright of Amherst County
Benjamin Wright		.08	1861 Benjamin Wright of Nelson County, son of 1816 Andrew Wright of Nelson County and grandson of William Wright (Amherst County)
James Wright		3.26	1839 James Wright of Nelson County, son of William Wright (Amherst County)
Danl L Wright		1.06	1882 Daniel L. Wright of Amherst County, son of 1850 Jesse Wright of Nelson County, grandson of 1799 Benjamin Wright of Amherst County, and great grandson of 1767 Francis Wright of Amherst County
Jesse Wright		1.06	1850 Jesse Wright of Nelson County, son of 1799 Benjamin Wright of Amherst County and grandson of 1767 Frances Wright of Amherst County
Wm Wright		.08	
Wm R Wright		.08	1871 William R. Wright of Buckingham County, son of 1842 Thomas Wright of Buckingham County
Nelson Wright			Nelson Wright, son of ____ Wright, grandson of 1839 James Wright of Nelson County, and great grandson of William Wright (Amherst County)

1840 PERSONAL PROPERTY TAX LIST

NELSON COUNTY, VIRGINIA

Appendix: Nelson County, Virginia, 1840 Personal Property Tax List:

District of John H Wingfield:

Date of receiving list of individuals		Number of White Males above 16 Years of age	Blacks above 12 and under 16 Years of age	Blacks above 16 Years of age	Horses Colts Mares & Mules	Stud Horses & Jack Asses	Rate of Covering pr Season	Coaches Chariots and Post Chases	Carriage Wheels		
									Other riding four Wheel Carriages	Riding Carriages with two Wheels	Value of each Carriage D C
March 3	Robert Wright	1			1						
March 3	Henry Wright	1									
March 20	Benja Wright	2			1						
March 23	Andrew W Wright	1			1						
March 23	John B Wright	1		1	1						
Apl 4	Danl L Wright	1	1	1	2						
Apl 4	Shelton Wright	1	1	2	4						
Apl 4	Jesse Wright	1		2	2						
Apl 14	William Wright (PR)	1			1						
Apl 15	Est James Wright		2	6	9						
Apl 15	John Wright	1									
Apl 18	William Wright (JR)	1			2						

Appendix: Nelson County, Virginia, 1840 Personal Property Tax List:

District of John H Wingfield:

[continued from prior page]	Tax on each Carriage	Sum Total of Taxes	Identification
Robert Wright		.08	1855 Robert M. Wright of Nelson County, son of Mary Wright, grandson of 1816 Andrew Wright of Nelson County, and great grandson of William Wright (Amherst County)
Henry Wright			
Benja Wright		.08	1861 Benjamin Wright of Nelson County, son of 1816 Andrew Wright of Nelson County and grandson of William Wright (Amherst County)
Andrew W Wright		.08	Andrew Washington Wright, son of 1861 Benjamin Wright of Nelson County, grandson of 1816 Andrew Wright of Nelson County, and great grandson of William Wright (Amherst County)
John B Wright		.38	John B. Wright, son of 1861 Benjamin Wright of Nelson County, grandson of 1816 Andrew Wright of Nelson County, and great grandson of William Wright (Amherst County)
Danl L Wright		.76	1882 Daniel L. Wright of Amherst County, son of 1850 Jesse Wright of Nelson County, grandson of 1799 Benjamin Wright of Amherst County, and great grandson of 1767 Francis Wright of Amherst County
Shelton Wright		1.22	1874 Shelton Wright of Nelson County, son of 1850 Jesse Wright of Nelson County, grandson of 1799 Benjamin Wright of Amherst County, and grandson of 1767 Francis Wright of Amherst County
Jesse Wright		.76	1850 Jesse Wright of Nelson County, son of 1799 Benjamin Wright of Amherst County and grandson of 1767 Frances Wright of Amherst County
William Wright (PR)		.08	
Est James Wright		3.12	Estate of 1839 James Wright of Nelson County, son of William Wright (Amherst County)
John Wright			John Wright, son of 1839 James Wright of Nelson County and grandson of William Wright (Amherst County)
William Wright (JR)		.16	

1841 PERSONAL PROPERTY TAX LIST

NELSON COUNTY, VIRGINIA

Appendix: Nelson County, Virginia, 1841 Personal Property Tax List:

District of John H Wingfield:

Date of receiving Lists of Individuals	Names of Individuals	No. of White Males above 16 years of age	Slaves above 12 years of age	Slaves above 16 years of age	Horses Colts Mares and Mules	Carriage Wheels			
						Coaches Chariots and Post Chaises	Other riding four Wheeled Carriages	Riding Carriages with Two Wheels	Value of each Carriage
March 18	Samuel B Wright	1			1				
March 18	Andrew W Wright	1			1				
March 18	Benjamin Wright	2		1	1				
March 25	Shelton Wright	1	2	1	5				
March 26	Daniel L Wright	1	1	2	2				
March 26	Jessee Wright	1		2	2				
March 26	William Wright	1			1				
April 3	John B Wright	1			1				
May 8	William H Wright	1							
May 12	William R Wright	1		1	2				
May 12	Thomas P Wright	1		2	1				
May 18	Est James Wright		2	6	6				
May 18	John Wright	1							

Appendix: Nelson County, Virginia, 1841 Personal Property Tax List:

District of John H Wingfield:

Names of Individuals [continued from prior page]	Tax on each Carriage	Amount of Taxes	Identification
Samuel B Wright		.12½	1907 Samuel Bell Wright of Roane County, West Virginia, son of 1861 Benjamin Wright of Nelson County, grandson of 1816 Andrew Wright of Nelson County, and great grandson of William Wright (Amherst County)
Andrew W Wright		.12½	Andrew Washington Wright, son of 1861 Benjamin Wright of Nelson County, grandson of 1816 Andrew Wright of Nelson County, and great grandson of William Wright (Amherst County)
Benjamin Wright		.52½	1861 Benjamin Wright of Nelson County, son of 1816 Andrew Wright of Nelson County and grandson of William Wright (Amherst County)
Shelton Wright		1.82½	1874 Shelton Wright of Nelson County, son of 1850 Jesse Wright of Nelson County, grandson of 1799 Benjamin Wright of Amherst County, and grandson of 1767 Francis Wright of Amherst County
Daniel L Wright		1.45	1882 Daniel L. Wright of Amherst County, son of 1850 Jesse Wright of Nelson County, grandson of 1799 Benjamin Wright of Amherst County, and great grandson of 1767 Francis Wright of Amherst County
Jessee Wright		1.05	1850 Jesse Wright of Nelson County, son of 1799 Benjamin Wright of Amherst County and grandson of 1767 Frances Wright of Amherst County
William Wright		.12½	
John B Wright		.12½	John B. Wright, son of 1861 Benjamin Wright of Nelson County, grandson of 1816 Andrew Wright of Nelson County, and great grandson of William Wright (Amherst County)
William H Wright			
William R Wright		.65	1871 William R. Wright of Buckingham County, son of 1842 Thomas Wright of Buckingham County
Thomas P Wright		.92½	
Est James Wright		3.95	Est of 1839 James Wright of Nelson County, son of William Wright (Amherst County)
John Wright			John Wright, son of 1839 James Wright of Nelson County and grandson of William Wright (Amherst County)

1842 PERSONAL PROPERTY TAX LIST

NELSON COUNTY, VIRGINIA

Appendix: Nelson County, Virginia, 1842 Personal Property Tax List:

District of Jno. H Wingfield:

Date of receiving lists of individuals		Number of White Males above 16 years of Age	Blacks above 12 & under 15 years of Age	Blacks Above 15 years of Age	Horses Mares Colts & Mules	Number of Metalick Clocks	Number of Gold Watches	Number of silver or other Metal Watches	Number of Piano Fortes	Value of each Piano Forte	Amt of silver & gold Plate Taxable	Phaetons & other 4 Wheel riding Carriages
	William R Wright	1		2	2	1						
	Thomas P Wright	1		2	2	1	1					
	Robert M Wright	1										
	William H Wright	1										
	Charles Wright	1			2							
	Shelton Wright	1	1	1	5							
	Daniel L Wright	1		3	3							
	Jesse Wright	1		1	1							

Appendix: Nelson County, Virginia, 1842 Personal Property Tax List:

District of Jno. H Wingfield:

[continued from prior page]	Carryalls jersey & Stage Waggons	Two wheel riding Carriages	Value of each Carriage	Tax on each Carriage	Sum Total of Taxes	Identification
William R Wright					1.55	1871 William R. Wright of Buckingham County, son of 1842 Thomas Wright of Buckingham County
Thomas P Wright					2.55	
Robert M Wright						1855 Robert M. Wright of Nelson County, son of Mary Wright, grandson of 1816 Andrew Wright of Nelson County, and great grandson of William Wright (Amherst County)
William H Wright						
Charles Wright					.25	1882 Charles H. Wright of Nelson County, son of Benjamin Wright, grandson of 1830 Moses Wright of Amherst County, great grandson of 1799 Benjamin Wright of Amherst County, and great great grandson of 1767 Francis Wright of Amherst County
Shelton Wright					1.42½	1874 Shelton Wright of Nelson County, son of 1850 Jesse Wright of Nelson County, grandson of 1799 Benjamin Wright of Amherst County, and grandson of 1767 Francis Wright of Amherst County
Daniel L Wright					1.57½	1882 Daniel L. Wright of Amherst County, son of 1850 Jesse Wright of Nelson County, grandson of 1799 Benjamin Wright of Amherst County, and great grandson of 1767 Francis Wright of Amherst County
Jesse Wright					.52½	1850 Jesse Wright of Nelson County, son of 1799 Benjamin Wright of Amherst County and grandson of 1767 Frances Wright of Amherst County

Appendix: Nelson County, Virginia, 1842 Personal Property Tax List:

District of Jno. H Wingfield:

Date of receiving lists of individuals		Number of White Males above 16 years of Age	Blacks above 12 & under 15 years of Age	Blacks Above 15 years of Age	Horses Mares Colts & Mules	Number of Metalick Clocks	Number of Gold Watches	Number of silver or other Metal Watches	Number of Piano Fortes	Value of each Piano Forte	Amt of silver & gold Plate Taxable	Phaetons & other 4 Wheel riding Carriages
	John B Wright	1			1			1				
	Nelson Wright	1										
	Andrew W Wright	1			1							
	Est James Wright	1	2	6	6	1		1				

164.

Appendix: Nelson County, Virginia, 1842 Personal Property Tax List:

District of Jno. H Wingfield:

[continued from prior page]	Carryalls jersey & Stage Waggons	Two wheel riding Carriages	Value of each Carriage	Tax on each Carriage	Sum Total of Taxes	Identification
John B Wright					.37½	John B. Wright, son of 1861 Benjamin Wright of Nelson County, grandson of 1816 Andrew Wright of Nelson County, and great grandson of William Wright (Amherst County)
Nelson Wright						Nelson Wright, son of ____ Wright, grandson of 1839 James Wright of Nelson County, and great grandson of William Wright (Amherst County)
Andrew W Wright					.12½	Andrew Washington Wright, son of 1861 Benjamin Wright of Nelson County, grandson of 1816 Andrew Wright of Nelson County, and great grandson of William Wright (Amherst County)
Est. James Wright					4.70	Estate of 1839 James Wright of Nelson County, son of William Wright (Amherst County)

1843 PERSONAL PROPERTY TAX LIST

NELSON COUNTY, VIRGINIA

Appendix: Nelson County, Virginia, 1843 Personal Property Tax List:

District of John H Wingfield:

Date of receiving lists of Individuals		Number of white Males above 16 years of age	Slaves above 12 and under 16 years of age	Slaves above 16 years of age	Horses Colts Mares & Mules	Number of Metalick Clocks	Number of Wooden Clocks	Number of Gold Watches	Number of silver lever & lupine Watches	Number of Metal Watches	Number of Medalick Watches	Phaetons and other 4 Wheel riding Carriages
Apl 8	Samuel B Wright	1										
Apl 8	William H Wright	1		1								
Apl 8	John B Wright	1		1	1		1					
Apl 8	Robert Wright	1										
Apl 17	Nelson Wright	1										
Apl 21	Daniel L Wright	1		1	2		1					
Apl 21	Jesse Wright	1		2	2							
May 2	Benjamin Wright	2			2		1					

Appendix: Nelson County, Virginia, 1843 Personal Property Tax List:

District of John H Wingfield:

[continued from prior page]	Carryalls jersey & Stage Waggons	Riding Carriages with 2 wheels	Value of each Carriage	Tax on each Carriage	Sum Total of Taxes	Identification
Samuel B Wright						1907 Samuel Bell Wright of Roane County, West Virginia, son of 1861 Benjamin Wright of Nelson County, grandson of 1816 Andrew Wright of Nelson County, and great grandson of William Wright (Amherst County)
William H Wright					.14	
John B Wright					.85	John B. Wright, son of 1861 Benjamin Wright of Nelson County, grandson of 1816 Andrew Wright of Nelson County, and great grandson of William Wright (Amherst County)
Robert Wright						1855 Robert M. Wright of Nelson County, son of Mary Wright, grandson of 1816 Andrew Wright of Nelson County, and great grandson of William Wright (Amherst County)
Nelson Wright					.10	Nelson Wright, son of ____ Wright, grandson of 1839 James Wright of Nelson County, and great grandson of William Wright (Amherst County)
Daniel L Wright					.99	1882 Daniel L. Wright of Amherst County, son of 1850 Jesse Wright of Nelson County, grandson of 1799 Benjamin Wright of Amherst County, and great grandson of 1767 Francis Wright of Amherst County
Jesse Wright					1.20	1850 Jesse Wright of Nelson County, son of 1799 Benjamin Wright of Amherst County and grandson of 1767 Frances Wright of Amherst County
Benjamin Wright					.53	1861 Benjamin Wright of Nelson County, son of 1816 Andrew Wright of Nelson County and grandson of William Wright (Amherst County)

1437(091908)

Appendix: Nelson County, Virginia, 1843 Personal Property Tax List:

District of John H Wingfield:

Date of receiving lists of Individuals		Number of white Males above 16 years of age	Slaves above 12 and under 16 years of age	Slaves above 16 years of age	Horses Colts Mares & Mules	Number of Metalick Clocks	Number of Wooden Clocks	Number of Gold Watches	Number of silver lever & lupine Watches	Number of Metal Watches	Number of Medalick Watches	Phaetons and other 4 Wheel riding Carriages
May 12	Charles Wright	1			1							
May 13	Shelton Wright	1	1	2	5		1					
May 22	Est James Wright	1	4	6	8	1						
May 26	William R Wright	1		1	2	1						
May 26	Thomas F Wright	1										
May 27	Andrew W Wright	1			2							

Appendix: Nelson County, Virginia, 1843 Personal Property Tax List:

District of John H Wingfield:

[continued from prior page]	Carryalls jersey & Stage Waggons	Riding Carriages with 2 wheels	Value of each Carriage	Tax on each Carriage	Sum Total of Taxes	Identification
Charles Wright					.14	1882 Charles H. Wright of Nelson County, son of Benjamin Wright, grandson of 1830 Moses Wright of Amherst County, great grandson of 1799 Benjamin Wright of Amherst County, and great great grandson of 1767 Francis Wright of Amherst County
Shelton Wright					2.33	1874 Shelton Wright of Nelson County, son of 1850 Jesse Wright of Nelson County, grandson of 1799 Benjamin Wright of Amherst County, and grandson of 1767 Francis Wright of Amherst County
Est James Wright					6.22	Estate of 1839 James Wright of Nelson County, son of William Wright (Amherst County)
William R Wright					1.24	1871 William R. Wright of Buckingham County, son of 1842 Thomas Wright of Buckingham County
Thomas F Wright						
Andrew W Wright					.28	Andrew Washington Wright, son of 1861 Benjamin Wright of Nelson County, grandson of 1816 Andrew Wright of Nelson County, and great grandson of William Wright (Amherst County)

1844 PERSONAL PROPERTY TAX LIST

NELSON COUNTY, VIRGINIA

Appendix: Nelson County, Virginia, 1844 Personal Property Tax List:

District of John H Wingfield:

Date of Receiving Lists	Persons Chargable with Tax	White males above 16 years	Slaves above 12 and under 16 years of age	Slaves above 16 years	Horses &c	Number of 4 wheel Pleasure Carriages and Value	Number of Stages and Value	Number of Carry-alls and Value	Number of 2 Wheel Pleasure Carriages and Value	Gold Watches	Silver, Patent levre or lupine Watches	Other Watches
Feby 29	Andrew W Wright	1			2							
Mar 20	Charles Wright	1			2							
Mar 25	John B Wright	1			3							
Mar 27	William R Wright	1		1	2							
Mar 30	Jesse Wright	1		2	2							
Mar 30	Daniel L Wright	1		1	2							
Apl 1	Shelton Wright	1		2	4							
Apl 1	James Wright	1			1							
Apl 13	Robert M Wright	1			1							
Apl 13	Nelson Wright	1										
Apl 13	Benjamin Wright	2			1							

Appendix: Nelson County, Virginia, 1844 Personal Property Tax List:

District of John H Wingfield:

Persons Chargable with Tax [continued from prior page]	Clocks at 50 Cents	Clocks at 25 Cents	Number of Pianos and Value	Gold and Silver plate	Attorneys paying Specific Tax and amount of Tax	Physicians and Surgeons paying Specific Tax and amount of Tax	Dentists paying Specific and Amount of Tax	Amount of interest or Profits on monies loaned out on bonds acquired by Purchase including interest profits or dividends on State or Corporation Bonds
Andrew W Wright								
Charles Wright								
John B Wright		1						
William R Wright								
Jesse Wright								
Daniel L Wright								
Shelton Wright								
James Wright								
Robert M Wright								
Nelson Wright								
Benjamin Wright		1						

Appendix: Nelson County, Virginia, 1844 Personal Property Tax List:

District of John H Wingfield:

Persons Chargable with Tax [continued from prior page]	Amount of monied yearly income over $400.00 received as salaries or Fees of office	Bridges amount of yearly rent or Value over $100.00	Ferries amount of yearly rent or Value over $100.00	Number of newspaper print-presses and Tax	Deed Probate offices and letters of administration	Total Amount of D C
Andrew W Wright						.25
Charles Wright						.25
John B Wright						
William R Wright						
Jesse Wright						1.05
Daniel L Wright						.90
Shelton Wright						
James Wright						
Robert M Wright						
Nelson Wright						
Benjamin Wright						

Appendix: Nelson County, Virginia, 1844 Personal Property Tax List:

District of John H Wingfield:

Persons Chargable with Tax [continued from prior page]	Identification
Andrew W Wright	Andrew Washington Wright, son of 1861 Benjamin Wright of Nelson County, grandson of 1816 Andrew Wright of Nelson County, and great grandson of William Wright (Amherst County)
Charles Wright	1882 Charles H. Wright of Nelson County, son of Benjamin Wright, grandson of 1830 Moses Wright of Amherst County, great grandson of 1799 Benjamin Wright of Amherst County, and great great grandson of 1767 Francis Wright of Amherst County
John B Wright	John B. Wright, son of 1861 Benjamin Wright of Nelson County, grandson of 1816 Andrew Wright of Nelson County, and great grandson of William Wright (Amherst County)
William R Wright	1871 William R. Wright of Buckingham County, son of 1842 Thomas Wright of Buckingham County
Jesse Wright	1850 Jesse Wright of Nelson County, son of 1799 Benjamin Wright of Amherst County and grandson of 1767 Frances Wright of Amherst County
Daniel L Wright	1882 Daniel L. Wright of Amherst County, son of 1850 Jesse Wright of Nelson County, grandson of 1799 Benjamin Wright of Amherst County, and great grandson of 1767 Francis Wright of Amherst County
Shelton Wright	1874 Shelton Wright of Nelson County, son of 1850 Jesse Wright of Nelson County, grandson of 1799 Benjamin Wright of Amherst County, and grandson of 1767 Francis Wright of Amherst County
James Wright	James Wright, son of Benjamin Wright, grandson of 1830 Moses Wright of Amherst County, great grandson of 1799 Benjamin Wright of Amherst County, and great great grandson of 1767 Francis Wright of Amherst County
Robert M Wright	1855 Robert M. Wright of Nelson County, son of Mary Wright, grandson of 1816 Andrew Wright of Nelson County, and great grandson of William Wright (Amherst County)
Nelson Wright	Nelson Wright, son of ____ Wright, grandson of 1839 James Wright of Nelson County, and great grandson of William Wright (Amherst County)
Benjamin Wright	1861 Benjamin Wright of Nelson County, son of 1816 Andrew Wright of Nelson County and grandson of William Wright (Amherst County)

Appendix: Nelson County, Virginia, 1844 Personal Property Tax List:

District of John H Wingfield:

Date of Receiving Lists	Persons Chargable with Tax	White males above 16 years	Slaves above 12 and under 16 years of age	Slaves above 16 years	Horses &c	Number of 4 wheel Pleasure Carriages and Value	Number of Stages and Value	Number of Carry-alls and Value	Number of 2 Wheel Pleasure Carriages and Value	Gold Watches	Silver, Patent levre or lupine Watches	Other Watches
Apl 13	Est James Wright	1	4	6	8							
Apl 13	Samuel B Wright	1			2							

Appendix: Nelson County, Virginia, 1844 Personal Property Tax List:

District of John H Wingfield:

Persons Chargable with Tax [continued from prior page]	Clocks at 50 Cents	Clocks at 25 Cents	Number of Pianos and Value	Gold and Silver plate	Attorneys paying Specific Tax and amount of Tax	Physicians and Surgeons paying Specific Tax and amount of Tax	Dentists paying Specific and Amount of Tax	Amount of interest or Profits on monies loaned out on bonds acquired by Purchase including interest profits or dividends on State or Corporation Bonds
Est James Wright								
Samuel B Wright								

Appendix: Nelson County, Virginia, 1844 Personal Property Tax List:

District of John H Wingfield:

Persons Chargable with Tax [continued from prior page]	Amount of monied yearly income over $400.00 received as salaries or Fees of office	Bridges amount of yearly rent or Value over $100.00	Ferries amount of yearly rent or Value over $100.00	Number of newspaper print-presses and Tax	Deed Probate offices and letters of administration	Total Amount of D C
Est James Wright						
Samuel B Wright						

Appendix: Nelson County, Virginia, 1844 Personal Property Tax List:

District of John H Wingfield:

Persons Chargable with Tax [continued from prior page]	Identification
Est James Wright	Estate of 1839 James Wright of Nelson County, son of William Wright (Amherst County)
Samuel B Wright	1907 Samuel Bell Wright of Roane County, West Virginia, son of 1861 Benjamin Wright of Nelson County, grandson of 1816 Andrew Wright of Nelson County, and great grandson of William Wright (Amherst County)

1845 PERSONAL PROPERTY TAX LIST

NELSON COUNTY, VIRGINIA

Appendix: Nelson County, Virginia, 1845 Personal Property Tax List:

District of Jno. H Wingfield:

Persons Chargeable with Tax	White males above 16 years of age	Slaves above 16 years of age	Slaves above 12 years of age	Horses, mules, &c	4 wheel pleasure carriages and harness, and value	Stages and value, including harness	Carry-alls and harness, and value	2 Wheel pleasure carriages and harness and value	Gold watches	Patent lever or lepine silver watches	Other Watches
Andrew W. Wright	1			1							
Benjamin Wright	2	1									
John B Wright	1			4							
Samuel B. Wright	1			2							
Shelton Wright	1	1		1							
Nelson Wright	1										

Appendix: Nelson County, Virginia, 1845 Personal Property Tax List:

District of John H Wingfield:

Persons Chargeable with Tax [continued from prior page]	Metallic clocks	Other clocks	Pianos, and value	Plate over the value of $50	Attorneys paying specific tax, and am't of tax	Physicians and surgeons paying specific tax, and amount of tax	Dentists paying specific tax, and amount of tax	Am't of int. or profits on moneys loaned out, or on bonds acquired by purchase, including interest, profits or dividends on state or corporat'n bonds
Andrew W. Wright								
Benjamin Wright		1						
John B Wright								
Samuel B. Wright								
Shelton Wright								
Nelson Wright								

Appendix: Nelson County, Virginia, 1845 Personal Property Tax List:

District of John H Wingfield:

Persons Chargable with Tax [continued from prior page]	Am't of monied yearly income over $400, received as salaries or fees of office	Bridges - am't of yearly rent or value over $100	Ferries - am't of yearly rent or value over $100	Newspaper printing presses, and amount of tax	Total am't of tax Dollars. Cents.	Identification
Andrew W. Wright					.10	Andrew Washington Wright, son of 1861 Benjamin Wright of Nelson County, grandson of 1816 Andrew Wright of Nelson County, and great grandson of William Wright (Amherst County)
Benjamin Wright					.44½	1861 Benjamin Wright of Nelson County, son of 1816 Andrew Wright of Nelson County and grandson of William Wright (Amherst County)
John B Wright					.40	John B. Wright, son of 1861 Benjamin Wright of Nelson County, grandson of 1816 Andrew Wright of Nelson County, and great grandson of William Wright (Amherst County)
Samuel B. Wright					.20	1907 Samuel Bell Wright of Roane County, West Virginia, son of 1861 Benjamin Wright of Nelson County, grandson of 1816 Andrew Wright of Nelson County, and great grandson of William Wright (Amherst County)
Shelton Wright					.42	1874 Shelton Wright of Nelson County, son of 1850 Jesse Wright of Nelson County, grandson of 1799 Benjamin Wright of Amherst County, and grandson of 1767 Francis Wright of Amherst County
Nelson Wright						Nelson Wright, son of ____ Wright, grandson of 1839 James Wright of Nelson County, and great grandson of William Wright (Amherst County)

Appendix: Nelson County, Virginia, 1845 Personal Property Tax List:

District of Jno. H Wingfield:

Persons Chargeable with Tax	White males above 16 years of age	Slaves above 16 years of age	Slaves above 12 years of age	Horses, mules, &c	4 wheel pleasure carriages and harness, and value	Stages and value, including harness	Carry-alls and harness, and value	2 Wheel pleasure carriages and harness and value	Gold watches	Patent lever or lepine silver watches	Other Watches
Robert M. Wright	1			1							
William H. Wright	1										
William R. Wright	1	3		2							
Charles Wright	1			3							
James Wright	1			1							
Jesse Wright	1	2		1							
Daniel L. Wright	1										

Appendix: Nelson County, Virginia, 1845 Personal Property Tax List:

District of John H Wingfield:

Persons Chargeable with Tax [continued from prior page]	Metallic clocks	Other clocks	Pianos, and value	Plate over the value of $50	Attorneys paying specific tax, and am't of tax	Physicians and surgeons paying specific tax, and amount of tax	Dentists paying specific tax, and amount of tax	Am't of int. or profits on moneys loaned out, or on bonds acquired by purchase, including interest, profits or dividends on state or corporat'n bonds
Robert M. Wright								
William H. Wright								
William R. Wright								
Charles Wright								
James Wright								
Jesse Wright								
Daniel L. Wright								

Appendix: Nelson County, Virginia, 1845 Personal Property Tax List:

District of John H Wingfield:

Persons Chargable with Tax [continued from prior page]	Am't of monied yearly income over $400, received as salaries or fees of office	Bridges - am't of yearly rent or value over $100	Ferries - am't of yearly rent or value over $100	Newspaper printing presses, and amount of tax	Total am't of tax Dollars. Cents.	Identification
Robert M. Wirght					.10	1855 Robert M. Wright of Nelson County, son of Mary Wright, grandson of 1816 Andrew Wright of Nelson County, and great grandson of William Wright (Amherst County)
William H. Wright						
William R. Wright					1.16	1871 William R. Wright of Buckingham County, son of 1842 Thomas Wright of Buckingham County
Charles Wright					.30	1882 Charles H. Wright of Nelson County, son of Benjamin Wright, grandson of 1830 Moses Wright of Amherst County, great grandson of 1799 Benjamin Wright of Amherst County, and great great grandson of 1767 Francis Wright of Amherst County
James Wright					.10	James Wright, son of Benjamin Wright, grandson of 1830 Moses Wright of Amherst County, great grandson of 1799 Benjamin Wright of Amherst County, and great great grandson of 1767 Francis Wright of Amherst County
Jesse Wright					.74	1850 Jesse Wright of Nelson County, son of 1799 Benjamin Wright of Amherst County and grandson of 1767 Frances Wright of Amherst County
Daniel L. Wright						1882 David L. Wright of Amherst County, son of 1850 Jesse Wright of Nelson County, grandson of 1799 Benjamin Wright of Amherst County, and great grandson of 1767 Francis Wright of Amherst County

Appendix: Nelson County, Virginia, 1845 Personal Property Tax List:

District of Jno. H Wingfield:

Persons Chargeable with Tax	White males above 16 years of age	Slaves above 16 years of age	Slaves above 12 years of age	Horses, mules, &c	4 wheel pleasure carriages and harness, and value	Stages and value, including harness	Carry-alls and harness, and value	2 Wheel pleasure carriages and harness and value	Gold watches	Patent lever or lepine silver watches	Other Watches
Est. James Wright	1	9	5	7							

Appendix: Nelson County, Virginia, 1845 Personal Property Tax List:

District of John H Wingfield:

Persons Chargeable with Tax [continued from prior page]	Metallic clocks	Other clocks	Pianos, and value	Plate over the value of $50	Attorneys paying specific tax, and am't of tax	Physicians and surgeons paying specific tax, and amount of tax	Dentists paying specific tax, and amount of tax	Am't of int. or profits on moneys loaned out, or on bonds acquired by purchase, including interest, profits or dividends on state or corporat'n bonds
Est. James Wright								

Appendix: Nelson County, Virginia, 1845 Personal Property Tax List:

District of John H Wingfield:

Persons Chargable with Tax [continued from prior page]	Am't of monied yearly income over $400, received as salaries or fees of office	Bridges - am't of yearly rent or value over $100	Ferries - am't of yearly rent or value over $100	Newspaper printing presses, and amount of tax	Total am't of tax Dollars. Cents.	Identification
Est. James Wright					5.18	Estate of 1839 James Wright of Nelson County, son of William Wright (Amherst County)

1846 PERSONAL PROPERTY TAX LIST

NELSON COUNTY, VIRGINIA

Appendix: Nelson County, Virginia, 1846 Personal Property Tax List:

District of John H. Wingfield:

Persons Chargeable with Tax	White males above 16 years of age	Slaves above 16 years of age	Slaves above 12 years of age	Horses, mules, &c	4 wheel pleasure carriages and harness, and value	Stages and value, including harness	Carry-alls and harness, and value	2 Wheel pleasure carriages and harness and value	Gold watches	Patent lever or lepine silver watches	Other Watches
John B Wright	1										
William H. Wright	1										
Robert M. Wright	1	1									
Nelson Wright	1										
Benjamin Wright	1	1		1							
Joseph A Wright	1										
Alexander Wright	1										
William Wright	1			1							

Appendix: Nelson County, Virginia, 1846 Personal Property Tax List:

District of John H. Wingfield:

Persons Chargeable with Tax [continued from prior page]	Metallic clocks	Other clocks	Pianos, and value	Plate over the value of $50	Attorneys paying specific tax, and am't of tax	Physicians and surgeons paying specific tax, and amount of tax	Dentists paying specific tax, and amount of tax	Am't of int. or profits on moneys loaned out, or on bonds acquired by purchase, including interest, profits or dividends on state or corporat'n bonds
John B Wright		1						
William H. Wright								
Robert M. Wright	1							
Nelson Wright								
Benjamin Wright		1						
Joseph A Wright								
Alexander Wright								
William Wright	1							

Appendix: Nelson County, Virginia, 1846 Personal Property Tax List:

District of John H. Wingfield:

Persons Chargable with Tax [continued from prior page]	Am't of monied yearly income over $400, received as salaries or fees of office	Bridges - am't of yearly rent or value over $100	Ferries - am't of yearly rent or value over $100	Newspaper printing presses, and amount of tax	Total am't of tax Dollars. Cents.	Identification
John B Wright					.12½	John B. Wright, son of 1861 Benjamin Wright of Nelson County, grandson of 1816 Andrew Wright of Nelson County, and great grandson of William Wright (Amherst County)
William H. Wright						
Robert M. Wright					.57	1855 Robert M. Wright of Nelson County, son of Mary Wright, grandson of 1816 Andrew Wright of Nelson County, and great grandson of William Wright (Amherst County)
Nelson Wright						Nelson Wright, son of ____ Wright, grandson of 1839 James Wright of Nelson County, and great grandson of William Wright (Amherst County)
Benjamin Wright					.54½	1861 Benjamin Wright of Nelson County, son of 1816 Andrew Wright of Nelson County and grandson of William Wright (Amherst County)
Joseph A Wright						
Alexander Wright						
William Wright					.35	

Appendix: Nelson County, Virginia, 1846 Personal Property Tax List:

District of John H. Wingfield:

Persons Chargeable with Tax	White males above 16 years of age	Slaves above 16 years of age	Slaves above 12 years of age	Horses, mules, &c	4 wheel pleasure carriages and harness, and value	Stages and value, including harness	Carry-alls and harness, and value	2 Wheel pleasure carriages and harness and value	Gold watches	Patent lever or lepine silver watches	Other Watches
Charles Wright	1			2							
Andrew W Wright	1			1							
Samuel B. Wright	1										
Nancy Wright		5		5					1		
Shelton Wright	1										
Daniel L Wright	1										

Appendix: Nelson County, Virginia, 1846 Personal Property Tax List:

District of John H. Wingfield:

Persons Chargeable with Tax [continued from prior page]	Metallic clocks	Other clocks	Pianos, and value	Plate over the value of $50	Attorneys paying specific tax, and am't of tax	Physicians and surgeons paying specific tax, and amount of tax	Dentists paying specific tax, and amount of tax	Am't of int. or profits on moneys loaned out, or on bonds acquired by purchase, including interest, profits or dividends on state or corporat'n bonds
Charles Wright								
Andrew W Wright								
Samuel B. Wright								
Nancy Wright								
Shelton Wright								
Daniel L Wright								

Appendix: Nelson County, Virginia, 1846 Personal Property Tax List:

District of John H. Wingfield:

Persons Chargable with Tax [continued from prior page]	Am't of monied yearly income over $400, received as salaries or fees of office	Bridges - am't of yearly rent or value over $100	Ferries - am't of yearly rent or value over $100	Newspaper printing presses, and amount of tax	Total am't of tax Dollars. Cents.	Identification
Charles Wright					.20	1882 Charles H. Wright of Nelson County, son of Benjamin Wright, grandson of 1830 Moses Wright of Amherst County, great grandson of 1799 Benjamin Wright of Amherst County, and great great grandson of 1767 Francis Wright of Amherst County
Andrew W Wright					.10	Andrew Washington Wright, son of 1861 Benjamin Wright of Nelson County, grandson of 1816 Andrew Wright of Nelson County, and great grandson of William Wright (Amherst County)
Samuel B. Wright						1907 Samuel Bell Wright of Roane County, West Virginia, son of 1861 Benjamin Wright of Nelson County, grandson of 1816 Andrew Wright of Nelson County, and great grandson of William Wright (Amherst County)
Nancy Wright					3.10	1851 William Wright of Amherst County
Shelton Wright						1874 Shelton Wright of Nelson County, son of 1850 Jesse Wright of Nelson County, grandson of 1799 Benjamin Wright of Amherst County, and grandson of 1767 Francis Wright of Amherst County
Daniel L Wright						1882 Daniel L. Wright of Amherst County, son of 1850 Jesse Wright of Nelson County, grandson of 1799 Benjamin Wright of Amherst County, and great grandson of 1767 Francis Wright of Amherst County

Appendix: Nelson County, Virginia, 1846 Personal Property Tax List:

District of John H. Wingfield:

Persons Chargeable with Tax	White males above 16 years of age	Slaves above 16 years of age	Slaves above 12 years of age	Horses, mules, &c	4 wheel pleasure carriages and harness, and value	Stages and value, including harness	Carry-alls and harness, and value	2 Wheel pleasure carriages and harness and value	Gold watches	Patent lever or lepine silver watches	Other Watches
Jessee Wright	1										
James Wright	1			1							
Est: Jas. Wright	1	9	5	8							

Appendix: Nelson County, Virginia, 1846 Personal Property Tax List:

District of John H. Wingfield:

Persons Chargeable with Tax [continued from prior page]	Metallic clocks	Other clocks	Pianos, and value	Plate over the value of $50	Attorneys paying specific tax, and am't of tax	Physicians and surgeons paying specific tax, and amount of tax	Dentists paying specific tax, and amount of tax	Am't of int. or profits on moneys loaned out, or on bonds acquired by purchase, including interest, profits or dividends on state or corporat'n bonds
Jessee Wright								
James Wright								
Est: Jas. Wright								

Appendix: Nelson County, Virginia, 1846 Personal Property Tax List:

District of John H. Wingfield:

Persons Chargable with Tax [continued from prior page]	Am't of monied yearly income over $400, received as salaries or fees of office	Bridges - am't of yearly rent or value over $100	Ferries - am't of yearly rent or value over $100	Newspaper printing presses, and amount of tax	Total am't of tax Dollars. Cents.	Identification
Jessee Wright						1850 Jesse Wright of Nelson County, son of 1799 Benjamin Wright of Amherst County and grandson of 1767 Frances Wright of Amherst County
James Wright					.10	James Wright, son of Benjamin Wright, grandson of 1830 Moses Wright of Amherst County, great grandson of 1799 Benjamin Wright of Amherst County, and great great grandson of 1767 Francis Wright of Amherst County
Est: Jas. Wright					5.28	Estate of 1839 James Wright of Nelson County, son of William Wright (Amherst County)

1847 PERSONAL PROPERTY TAX LIST

NELSON COUNTY, VIRGINIA

Appendix: Nelson County, Virginia, 1847 Personal Property Tax List:

District of John H. Wingfield:

Persons Chargeable with Tax	White males above 16 years of age	Slaves above 16 years of age	Slaves above 12 years of age	Horses, mules, &c	4 wheel pleasure carriages and harness, and value	Stages and value, including harness	Carry-alls and harness, and value	2 Wheel pleasure carriages and harness and value	Gold watches	Patent lever or lepine silver watches	Other Watches
Robert M Wright	1										
Samuel B Wright	1										
John B Wright	1	2									
Charles Wright	1			1							
Nancy Wright		4		3							
Jesse Wright	1										

Appendix: Nelson County, Virginia, 1847 Personal Property Tax List:

District of John H. Wingfield:

Persons Chargeable with Tax [continued from prior page]	Metallic clocks	Other clocks	Pianos, and value	Plate over the value of $50	Attorneys paying specific tax, and am't of tax	Physicians and surgeons paying specific tax, and amount of tax	Dentists paying specific tax, and amount of tax	Am't of int. or profits on moneys loaned out, or on bonds acquired by purchase, including interest, profits or dividends on state or corporat'n bonds
Robert M Wright	1							
Samuel B Wright								
John B Wright	1							
Charles Wright								
Nancy Wright	1							
Jesse Wright								

Appendix: Nelson County, Virginia, 1847 Personal Property Tax List:

District of John H. Wingfield:

Persons Chargable with Tax [continued from prior page]	Am't of monied yearly income over $400, received as salaries or fees of office	Bridges - am't of yearly rent or value over $100	Ferries - am't of yearly rent or value over $100	Newspaper printing presses, and amount of tax	Total am't of tax Dollars. Cents.	Identification
Robert M Wright					.25	1855 Robert M. Wright of Nelson County, son of Mary Wright, grandson of 1816 Andrew Wright of Nelson County, and great grandson of William Wright (Amherst County)
Samuel B Wright						1907 Samuel Bell Wright of Roane County, West Virginia, son of 1861 Benjamin Wright of Nelson County, grandson of 1816 Andrew Wright of Nelson County, and great grandson of William Wright (Amherst County)
John B Wright					.76½	John B. Wright, son of 1861 Benjamin Wright of Nelson County, grandson of 1816 Andrew Wright of Nelson County, and great grandson of William Wright (Amherst County)
Charles Wright					.10	1882 Charles H. Wright of Nelson County, son of Benjamin Wright, grandson of 1830 Moses Wright of Amherst County, great grandson of 1799 Benjamin Wright of Amherst County, and great great grandson of 1767 Francis Wright of Amherst County
Nancy Wright					1.70½	
Jesse Wright						1850 Jesse Wright of Nelson County, son of 1799 Benjamin Wright of Amherst County and grandson of 1767 Frances Wright of Amherst County

Appendix: Nelson County, Virginia, 1847 Personal Property Tax List:

District of John H. Wingfield:

Persons Chargeable with Tax	White males above 16 years of age	Slaves above 16 years of age	Slaves above 12 years of age	Horses, mules, &c	4 wheel pleasure carriages and harness, and value	Stages and value, including harness	Carry-alls and harness, and value	2 Wheel pleasure carriages and harness and value	Gold watches	Patent lever or lepine silver watches	Other Watches
Shelton Wright	1										
Daniel L Wright	1										
James Wright	1			1							
Robert Wright	1			1							1
Benjamin Wright	1	1									
Robert K Wright	1			1					1		
Andrew W Wright	1			1							

Appendix: Nelson County, Virginia, 1847 Personal Property Tax List:

District of John H. Wingfield:

Persons Chargeable with Tax [continued from prior page]	Metallic clocks	Other clocks	Pianos, and value	Plate over the value of $50	Attorneys paying specific tax, and am't of tax	Physicians and surgeons paying specific tax, and amount of tax	Dentists paying specific tax, and amount of tax	Am't of int. or profits on moneys loaned out, or on bonds acquired by purchase, including interest, profits or dividends on state or corporat'n bonds
Shelton Wright								
Daniel L Wright								
James Wright								
Robert Wright								
Benjamin Wright		1						
Robert K Wright								
Andrew W Wright								

Appendix: Nelson County, Virginia, 1847 Personal Property Tax List:

District of John H. Wingfield:

Persons Chargable with Tax [continued from prior page]	Am't of monied yearly income over $400, received as salaries or fees of office	Bridges - am't of yearly rent or value over $100	Ferries - am't of yearly rent or value over $100	Newspaper printing presses, and amount of tax	Total am't of tax Dollars. Cents.	Identification
Shelton Wright						1874 Shelton Wright of Nelson County, son of 1850 Jesse Wright of Nelson County, grandson of 1799 Benjamin Wright of Amherst County, and grandson of 1767 Francis Wright of Amherst County
Daniel L Wright						1882 Daniel L. Wright of Amherst County, son of 1850 Jesse Wright of Nelson County, grandson of 1799 Benjamin Wright of Amherst County, and great grandson of 1767 Francis Wright of Amherst County
James Wright					.10	James Wright, son of Benjamin Wright, grandson of 1830 Moses Wright of Amherst County, great grandson of 1799 Benjamin Wright of Amherst County, and great great grandson of 1767 Francis Wright of Amherst County
Robert Wright					.35	
Benjamin Wright					.44½	1861 Benjamin Wright of Nelson County, son of 1816 Andrew Wright of Nelson County and grandson of William Wright (Amherst County)
Robert K Wright					.10	1881 Robert Kincaid Wright of Roane County, West Virginia, son of 1861 Benjamin Wright of Nelson County, grandson of 1816 Andrew Wright of Nelson County, and great grandson of William Wright (Amherst County)
Andrew W Wright					.10	Andrew Washington Wright, son of 1861 Benjamin Wright of Nelson County, grandson of 1816 Andrew Wright of Nelson County, and great grandson of William Wright (Amherst County)

Appendix: Nelson County, Virginia, 1847 Personal Property Tax List:

District of John H. Wingfield:

Persons Chargeable with Tax	White males above 16 years of age	Slaves above 16 years of age	Slaves above 12 years of age	Horses, mules, &c	4 wheel pleasure carriages and harness, and value	Stages and value, including harness	Carry-alls and harness, and value	2 Wheel pleasure carriages and harness and value	Gold watches	Patent lever or lepine silver watches	Other Watches
Est Jas Wright	1	11		8							
Alexander Wright	1										
Nelson Wright	1										

Appendix: Nelson County, Virginia, 1847 Personal Property Tax List:

District of John H. Wingfield:

Persons Chargeable with Tax [continued from prior page]	Metallic clocks	Other clocks	Pianos, and value	Plate over the value of $50	Attorneys paying specific tax, and am't of tax	Physicians and surgeons paying specific tax, and amount of tax	Dentists paying specific tax, and amount of tax	Am't of int. or profits on moneys loaned out, or on bonds acquired by purchase, including interest, profits or dividends on state or corporat'n bonds
Est Jas Wright	1							
Alexander Wright								
Nelson Wright								

Appendix: Nelson County, Virginia, 1847 Personal Property Tax List:

District of John H. Wingfield:

Persons Chargable with Tax [continued from prior page]	Am't of monied yearly income over $400, received as salaries or fees of office	Bridges - am't of yearly rent or value over $100	Ferries - am't of yearly rent or value over $100	Newspaper printing presses, and amount of tax	Total am't of tax Dollars. Cents.	Identification
Est Jas Wright					4.51	Estate of 1839 James Wright of Nelson County, son of William Wright (Amherst County)
Alexander Wright						
Nelson Wright						Nelson Wright, son of _____ Wright, grandson of 1839 James Wright of Nelson County, and great grandson of William Wright (Amherst County)

1848 PERSONAL PROPERTY TAX LIST

NELSON COUNTY, VIRGINIA

Appendix: Nelson County, Virginia, 1848 Personal Property Tax List:

District of John H. Wingfield:

Persons Chargeable with Tax	White males above 16 years of age	Slaves above 16 years of age	Slaves above 12 years of age	Horses, mules, &c	4 wheel pleasure carriages and harness, and value	Stages and value, including harness	Carry-alls and harness, and value	2 Wheel pleasure carriages and harness and value	Gold watches	Patent lever or lepine silver watches	Other Watches
Robert M Wright	1										
Benjamin Wright	1										
Charles Wright	1			1							
John B Wright	1		1								1
James Wright	1			2							
Alexander Wright	1										
Est James Wright	1	8	12	6							

214.

Appendix: Nelson County, Virginia, 1848 Personal Property Tax List:

District of John H. Wingfield:

Persons Chargeable with Tax [continued from prior page]	Metallic clocks	Other clocks	Pianos, and value	Plate over the value of $50	Attorneys paying specific tax, and am't of tax	Physicians and surgeons paying specific tax, and amount of tax	Dentists paying specific tax, and amount of tax	Am't of int. or profits on moneys loaned out, or on bonds acquired by purchase, including interest, profits or dividends on state or corporat'n bonds
Robert M Wright	1							
Benjamin Wright		1						
Charles Wright								
John B Wright		1						
James Wright		1						
Alexander Wright								
Est James Wright		1						

Appendix: Nelson County, Virginia, 1848 Personal Property Tax List:

District of John H. Wingfield:

Persons Chargable with Tax [continued from prior page]	Am't of monied yearly income over $400, received as salaries or fees of office	Bridges - am't of yearly rent or value over $100	Ferries - am't of yearly rent or value over $100	Newspaper printing presses, and amount of tax	Total am't of tax Dollars. Cents.	Identification
Robert M Wright					.25	1855 Robert M. Wright of Nelson County, son of Mary Wright, grandson of 1816 Andrew Wright of Nelson County, and great grandson of William Wright (Amherst County)
Benjamin Wright					.12½	1861 Benjamin Wright of Nelson County, son of 1816 Andrew Wright of Nelson County and grandson of William Wright (Amherst County)
Charles Wright					.10	1882 Charles H. Wright of Nelson County, son of Benjamin Wright, grandson of 1830 Moses Wright of Amherst County, great grandson of 1799 Benjamin Wright of Amherst County, and great great grandson of 1767 Francis Wright of Amherst County
John B Wright					.69½	John B. Wright, son of 1861 Benjamin Wright of Nelson County, grandson of 1816 Andrew Wright of Nelson County, and great grandson of William Wright (Amherst County)
James Wright					.20	James Wright, son of Benjamin Wright, grandson of 1830 Moses Wright of Amherst County, great grandson of 1799 Benjamin Wright of Amherst County, and great great grandson of 1767 Francis Wright of Amherst County
Alexander Wright						
Est James Wright					4.69	Estate of 1839 James Wright of Nelson County, son of William Wright (Amherst County)

Appendix: Nelson County, Virginia, 1848 Personal Property Tax List:

District of John H. Wingfield:

Persons Chargeable with Tax [continued from prior page]	Metallic clocks	Other clocks	Pianos, and value	Plate over the value of $50	Attorneys paying specific tax, and am't of tax	Physicians and surgeons paying specific tax, and amount of tax	Dentists paying specific tax, and amount of tax	Am't of int. or profits on moneys loaned out, or on bonds acquired by purchase, including interest, profits or dividends on state or corporat'n bonds
Nelson Wright	1			1				

Appendix: Nelson County, Virginia, 1848 Personal Property Tax List:

District of John H. Wingfield:

Persons Chargeable with Tax [continued from prior page]	Metallic clocks	Other clocks	Pianos, and value	Plate over the value of $50	Attorneys paying specific tax, and am't of tax	Physicians and surgeons paying specific tax, and amount of tax	Dentists paying specific tax, and amount of tax	Am't of int. or profits on moneys loaned out, or on bonds acquired by purchase, including interest, profits or dividends on state or corporat'n bonds
Nelson Wright								

Appendix: Nelson County, Virginia, 1848 Personal Property Tax List:

District of John H. Wingfield:

Persons Chargable with Tax [continued from prior page]	Am't of monied yearly income over $400, received as salaries or fees of office	Bridges - am't of yearly rent or value over $100	Ferries - am't of yearly rent or value over $100	Newspaper printing presses, and amount of tax	Total am't of tax Dollars. Cents.	Identification
Nelson Wright					.10	Nelson Wright, son of ____ Wright, grandson of 1839 James Wright of Nelson County, and great grandson of William Wright (Amherst County)

Appendix: Nelson County, Virginia, 1848 Personal Property Tax List:

District of John H. Wingfield:

Persons Chargeable with Tax	White males above 16 years of age	Slaves above 16 years of age	Slaves above 12 years of age	Horses, mules, &c	4 wheel pleasure carriages and harness, and value	Stages and value, including harness	Carry-alls and harness, and value	2 Wheel pleasure carriages and harness and value	Gold watches	Patent lever or lepine silver watches	Other Watches
Andrew W Wright	1			1							
Nancy Wright		4	4	2							
Jesse Wright	1										
Robert K. Wright	1			1							

Appendix: Nelson County, Virginia, 1848 Personal Property Tax List:

District of John H. Wingfield:

Persons Chargeable with Tax [continued from prior page]	Metallic clocks	Other clocks	Pianos, and value	Plate over the value of $50	Attorneys paying specific tax, and am't of tax	Physicians and surgeons paying specific tax, and amount of tax	Dentists paying specific tax, and amount of tax	Am't of int. or profits on moneys loaned out, or on bonds acquired by purchase, including interest, profits or dividends on state or corporat'n bonds
Andrew W Wright								
Nancy Wright								
Jesse Wright								
Robert K. Wright								

1437(091908)

Appendix: Nelson County, Virginia, 1848 Personal Property Tax List:

District of John H. Wingfield:

Persons Chargable with Tax [continued from prior page]	Am't of monied yearly income over $400, received as salaries or fees of office	Bridges - am't of yearly rent or value over $100	Ferries - am't of yearly rent or value over $100	Newspaper printing presses, and amount of tax	Total am't of tax Dollars. Cents.	Identification
Andrew W. Wright					.10	Andrew Washington Wright, son of 1861 Benjamin Wright of Nelson County, grandson of 1816 Andrew Wright of Nelson County, and great grandson of William Wright (Amherst County)
Nancy Wright					1.48	
Jesse Wright						1850 Jesse Wright of Nelson County, son of 1799 Benjamin Wright of Amherst County and grandson of 1767 Frances Wright of Amherst County
Robert K Wright					.10	1881 Robert Kincaid Wright of Roane County, West Virginia, son of 1861 Benjamin Wright of Nelson County, grandson of 1816 Andrew Wright of Nelson County, and great grandson of William Wright (Amherst County)

1437(091908)

1849 PERSONAL PROPERTY TAX LIST

NELSON COUNTY, VIRGINIA

Appendix: Nelson County, Virginia, 1849 Personal Property Tax List:

District of John H. Wingfield:

Persons Chargeable with Tax	White males above 16 years of age	Slaves above 16 years of age	Slaves above 12 years of age	Horses, mules, &c	4 wheel pleasure carriages and harness, and value	Stages and value, including harness	Carry-alls and harness, and value	2 Wheel pleasure carriages and harness and value	Gold watches	Patent lever or lepine silver watches	Other Watches
Andrew W Wright	1			1							
William H Wright	1										
John B Wright	1		1								1
Robert M Wright	1										
Robert K Wright	1			1							
Moses Wright	1										
Robert Wright	1									1	

Appendix: Nelson County, Virginia, 1849 Personal Property Tax List:

District of John H. Wingfield:

Persons Chargeable with Tax [continued from prior page]	Metallic clocks	Other clocks	Pianos, and value	Plate over the value of $50	Attorneys paying specific tax, and am't of tax	Physicians and surgeons paying specific tax, and amount of tax	Dentists paying specific tax, and amount of tax	Am't of int. or profits on moneys loaned out, or on bonds acquired by purchase, including interest, profits or dividends on state or corporat'n bonds
Andrew W Wright								
William H Wright		1						
John B Wright		1						
Robert M Wright		1						
Robert K Wright								
Moses Wright								
Robert Wright								

Appendix: Nelson County, Virginia, 1849 Personal Property Tax List:

District of John H. Wingfield:

Persons Chargable with Tax [continued from prior page]	Am't of monied yearly income over $400, received as salaries or fees of office	Bridges - am't of yearly rent or value over $100	Ferries - am't of yearly rent or value over $100	Newspaper printing presses, and amount of tax	Total am't of tax Dollars. Cents.	Identification
Andrew W Wright					.10	Andrew Washington Wright, son of 1861 Benjamin Wright of Nelson County, grandson of 1816 Andrew Wright of Nelson County, and great grandson of William Wright (Amherst County)
William H Wright					.12½	
John B Wright					.69½	John B. Wright, son of 1861 Benjamin Wright of Nelson County, grandson of 1816 Andrew Wright of Nelson County, and great grandson of William Wright (Amherst County)
Robert M Wright					.25	1855 Robert M. Wright of Nelson County, son of Mary Wright, grandson of 1816 Andrew Wright of Nelson County, and great grandson of William Wright (Amherst County)
Robert K Wright					.10	1881 Robert Kincaid Wright of Roane County, West Virginia, son of 1861 Benjamin Wright of Nelson County, grandson of 1816 Andrew Wright of Nelson County, and great grandson of William Wright (Amherst County)
Moses Wright						1849 Moses Wright of Nelson County, son of 1830 Moses Wright of Amherst County, grandson of 1799 Benjamin Wright of Amherst County, and great grandson of 1767 Francis Wright of Amherst County
Robert Wright					.25	

Appendix: Nelson County, Virginia, 1849 Personal Property Tax List:

District of John H. Wingfield:

Persons Chargeable with Tax	White males above 16 years of age	Slaves above 16 years of age	Slaves above 12 years of age	Horses, mules, &c	4 wheel pleasure carriages and harness, and value	Stages and value, including harness	Carry-alls and harness, and value	2 Wheel pleasure carriages and harness and value	Gold watches	Patent lever or lepine silver watches	Other Watches
Nancy Wright		4	4	2							
Jessee Wright	1										
James Wright	1			2							
Alexander Wright	1			1							
Charles Wright	1			1							
Est James Wright	1	8	10	6							
Benjamin Wright	1			1							

Appendix: Nelson County, Virginia, 1849 Personal Property Tax List:

District of John H. Wingfield:

Persons Chargeable with Tax [continued from prior page]	Metallic clocks	Other clocks	Pianos, and value	Plate over the value of $50	Attorneys paying specific tax, and am't of tax	Physicians and surgeons paying specific tax, and amount of tax	Dentists paying specific tax, and amount of tax	Am't of int. or profits on moneys loaned out, or on bonds acquired by purchase, including interest, profits or dividends on state or corporat'n bonds
Nancy Wright		1						
Jessee Wright								
James Wright								
Alexander Wright								
Charles Wright								
Est James Wright	1							
Benjamin Wright		1						

1437(091908)

228.

Appendix: Nelson County, Virginia, 1849 Personal Property Tax List:

District of John H. Wingfield:

Persons Chargable with Tax [continued from prior page]	Am't of monied yearly income over $400, received as salaries or fees of office	Bridges - am't of yearly rent or value over $100	Ferries - am't of yearly rent or value over $100	Newspaper printing presses, and amount of tax	Total am't of tax Dollars. Cents.	Identification
Nancy Wright					1.60½	Nancy Wright, daughter of 1850 Jesse Wright of Nelson County, granddaughter of 1799 Benjamin Wright of Amherst County, and great granddaughter of 1767 Francis Wright of Amherst County
Jessee Wright						1850 Jesse Wright of Nelson County, son of 1799 Benjamin Wright of Amherst County and grandson of 1767 Frances Wright of Amherst County
James Wright					.20	James Wright, son of Benjamin Wright, grandson of 1830 Moses Wright of Amherst County, great grandson of 1799 Benjamin Wright of Amherst County, and great great grandson of 1767 Francis Wright of Amherst County
Alexander Wright					.10	
Charles Wright					.10	1882 Charles H. Wright of Nelson County, son of Benjamin Wright, grandson of 1830 Moses Wright of Amherst County, great grandson of 1799 Benjamin Wright of Amherst County, and great great grandson of 1767 Francis Wright of Amherst County
Est James Wright					4.05	1839 James Wright of Nelson County, son of William Wright (Amherst County)
Benjamin Wright					.22½	1861 Benjamin Wright of Nelson County, son of 1816 Andrew Wright of Nelson County and grandson of William Wright (Amherst County)

Appendix: Nelson County, Virginia, 1849 Personal Property Tax List:

District of John H. Wingfield:

Persons Chargeable with Tax	White males above 16 years of age	Slaves above 16 years of age	Slaves above 12 years of age	Horses, mules, &c	4 wheel pleasure carriages and harness, and value	Stages and value, including harness	Carry-alls and harness, and value	2 Wheel pleasure carriages and harness and value	Gold watches	Patent lever or lepine silver watches	Other Watches
Nelson Wright	1			1							

Appendix: Nelson County, Virginia, 1849 Personal Property Tax List:

District of John H. Wingfield:

Persons Chargeable with Tax [continued from prior page]	Metallic clocks	Other clocks	Pianos, and value	Plate over the value of $50	Attorneys paying specific tax, and am't of tax	Physicians and surgeons paying specific tax, and amount of tax	Dentists paying specific tax, and amount of tax	Am't of int. or profits on moneys loaned out, or on bonds acquired by purchase, including interest, profits or dividends on state or corporat'n bonds
Nelson Wright								

Appendix: Nelson County, Virginia, 1849 Personal Property Tax List:

District of John H. Wingfield:

Persons Chargable with Tax [continued from prior page]	Am't of monied yearly income over $400, received as salaries or fees of office	Bridges - am't of yearly rent or value over $100	Ferries - am't of yearly rent or value over $100	Newspaper printing presses, and amount of tax	Total am't of tax Dollars. Cents.	Identification
Nelson Wright					.10	Nelson Wright, son of ____ Wright, grandson of 1839 James Wright of Nelson County, and great grandson of William Wright (Amherst County)

1850 PERSONAL PROPERTY TAX LIST

NELSON COUNTY, VIRGINIA

Appendix: Nelson County, Virginia, 1850 Personal Property Tax List:

District of John H. Wingfield:

Persons Chargeable with Tax	White males above 16 years of age	Male free negroes above sixteen	Slaves above 16 years of age	Slaves above 12 years of age	Horses, mules, &c	4 wheel pleasure carriages and harness, and value	Stages and value, including harness	Carry-alls and harness, and value	2 Wheel pleasure carriages and harness and value	Gold watches	Patent lever or lepine silver watches	Other Watches
Robert M Wright	1											
Benjamin Wright	1				1							
Andrew W Wright	1				1							
Charles Wright	1				1							
Richard Wright	1											
Robert K Wright	1				1							
John B Wright	1		1	1								

Appendix: Nelson County, Virginia, 1850 Personal Property Tax List:

District of John H. Wingfield:

Persons Chargeable with Tax [continued from prior page]	Metallic clocks	Other clocks	Pianos, and value	Plate over the value of $50	Attorneys paying specific tax, and am't of tax	Physicians and surgeons paying specific tax, and amount of tax	Dentists paying specific tax, and amount of tax	Am't of int. or profits on moneys loaned out, or on bonds acquired by purchase, including interest, profits or dividends on state or corporat'n bonds
Robert M Wright	1							
Benjamin Wright		1						
Andrew W Wright	1							
Charles Wright								
Richard Wright								
Robert K Wright								
John B Wright								

Appendix: Nelson County, Virginia, 1850 Personal Property Tax List:

District of John H. Wingfield:

Persons Chargable with Tax [continued from prior page]	Am't of monied yearly income over $400, received as salaries or fees of office	Bridges - am't of yearly rent or value over $100	Ferries - am't of yearly rent or value over $100	Newspaper printing presses, and amount of tax	Total am't of tax Dollars. Cents.	Identification
Robert M Wright					.25	1855 Robert M. Wright of Nelson County, son of Mary Wright, grandson of 1816 Andrew Wright of Nelson County, and great grandson of William Wright (Amherst County)
Benjamin Wright					.22½	1861 Benjamin Wright of Nelson County, son of 1816 Andrew Wright of Nelson County and grandson of William Wright (Amherst County)
Andrew W Wright					.35	Andrew Washington Wright, son of 1861 Benjamin Wright of Nelson County, grandson of 1816 Andrew Wright of Nelson County, and great grandson of William Wright (Amherst County)
Charles Wright					.10	Charles Wright, son of Benjamin Wright, grandson of 1830 Moses Wright of Amherst County, great grandson of 1799 Benjamin Wright of Amherst County, and great great grandson of 1767 Francis Wright of Amherst County
Richard Wright						
Robert K Wright					.10	1881 Robert Kincaid Wright of Roane County, West Virginia, son of 1861 Benjamin Wright of Nelson County, grandson of 1816 Andrew Wright of Nelson County, and great grandson of William Wright (Amherst County)
John B Wright					.32	John B. Wright, son of 1861 Benjamin Wright of Nelson County, grandson of 1816 Andrew Wright of Nelson County, and great grandson of William Wright (Amherst County)

Appendix: Nelson County, Virginia, 1850 Personal Property Tax List:

District of John H. Wingfield:

Persons Chargeable with Tax	White males above 16 years of age	Male free negroes above sixteen	Slaves above 16 years of age	Slaves above 12 years of age	Horses, mules, &c	4 wheel pleasure carriages and harness, and value	Stages and value, including harness	Carry-alls and harness, and value	2 Wheel pleasure carriages and harness and value	Gold watches	Patent lever or lepine silver watches	Other Watches
Nelson Wright	1				1							
Nancy Wright			4	4	2							
Jesse Wright	1											
Mary Wright			5	6	4							
Robert Wright	1											1
William H Wright	1											

Appendix: Nelson County, Virginia, 1850 Personal Property Tax List:

District of John H. Wingfield:

Persons Chargeable with Tax [continued from prior page]	Metallic clocks	Other clocks	Pianos, and value	Plate over the value of $50	Attorneys paying specific tax, and am't of tax	Physicians and surgeons paying specific tax, and amount of tax	Dentists paying specific tax, and amount of tax	Am't of int. or profits on moneys loaned out, or on bonds acquired by purchase, including interest, profits or dividends on state or corporat'n bonds
Nelson Wright								
Nancy Wright			1					
Jessee Wright								
Mary Wright	1							
Robert Wright								
William H Wright			1					

238.

Appendix: Nelson County, Virginia, 1850 Personal Property Tax List:

District of John H. Wingfield:

Persons Chargable with Tax [continued from prior page]	Am't of monied yearly income over $400, received as salaries or fees of office	Bridges - am't of yearly rent or value over $100	Ferries - am't of yearly rent or value over $100	Newspaper printing presses, and amount of tax	Total am't of tax Dollars. Cents.	Identification
Nelson Wright					.10	Nelson Wright, son of ____ Wright, grandson of 1839 James Wright of Nelson County, and great grandson of William Wright (Amherst County)
Nancy Wright					1.60½	Nancy Wright, daughter of 1850 Jesse Wright of Nelson County, granddaughter of 1799 Benjamin Wright of Amherst County, and great granddaughter of 1767 Francis Wright of Amherst County
Jessee Wright						1850 Jesse Wright of Nelson County, son of 1799 Benjamin Wright of Amherst County and grandson of 1767 Frances Wright of Amherst County
Mary Wright					2.57	Mary "Polly" Wright, daughter of 1839 James Wright of Nelson County and granddaughter of William Wright (Amherst County)
Robert Wright					.25	
William H Wright					.12½	

INDEX

Wright, Alec, 12
Wright, Alex, 16, 20, 31, 32, 33, 34, 35, 36, 37, 40, 41
Wright, Alexander, 48, 49, 54, 55, 194, 195, 196, 210 211, 212, 214, 215, 216, 227, 228, 229
Wright, Alexr., 8
Wright, Alxr., 2
Wright, Andrew, 2, 8, 12, 16, 21, 24, 25, 26, 27, 28, 29, 30, 40, 41, 82, 83, 88, 89, 100, 101,
Wright, Andrew W, 108, 109, 114, 115, 120, 121, 124, 125, 130, 131, 134, 135, 140, 141, 144, 145, 150, 15, 154, 155, 158, 159, 164, 165, 170, 171, 174, 175, 176, 177, 184, 185, 186, 197, 198, 199, 207, 208, 209, 220, 221, 222, 224, 225, 226, 234, 235, 236
Wright, Archillis, 2
Wright, Austin, 2, 12, 16, 20, 24, 25, 26, 27, 28, 29, 30, 31, 32, 33, 34, 35, 36, 37, 40, 41, 44, 45, 48, 49, 54, 55, 62, 63, 66, 67, 70, 71, 74, 75, 78, 79, 82, 83, 90, 91, 94, 95, 100, 101, 108, 109, 114, 115, 120, 121, 126, 127, 134, 135, 140, 141, 146, 147
Wright Jr, Austin, 40, 41, 48, 49
Wright, Ben, 16, 21, 24, 25, 26, 27, 28, 29, 30
Wright, Benj, 2, 12, 40, 41, 44, 45, 48, 49
Wright, Benja, 154, 155
Wright, Benjamin, 54, 55, 58, 59, 62, 63, 66, 67, 70, 71, 74, 75, 78, 79, 82, 83, 88, 89, 94, 95, 102, 103, 108, 109, 114, 115, 120, 121, 124, 125, 130, 131, 134, 135, 140, 141, 144, 145, 150, 151, 158, 159, 168, 19, 174, 175, 176, 177, 184, 185, 186, 194, 195, 196, 207, 208, 209, 214, 215, 216, 227, 228, 229, 234, 235, 236
Wright, Benjn, 8
Wright, Bennet, 108, 109, 116, 117
Wright, Bennett, 94, 95, 100, 101

Wright, Charles, 90, 91, 144, 145, 162, 163, 170, 171, 174, 175, 176, 177, 187, 188, 189, 197, 198, 199, 204, 205, 206, 214, 215, 216, 227, 228, 229, 234, 235, 236
Wright, Chas, 150, 151
Wright, Daniel L, 120, 121, 136, 137, 144, 145, 158, 159, 162, 163, 168, 169, 174, 175, 176, 177, 187, 188, 189, 197, 198, 199, 207, 208, 209
Wright, Danl L, 140, 141, 150, 151, 154, 155
Wright, Ellis, 74, 75, 78, 79, 82, 83, 88, 89, 94, 95, 100, 1001, 110, 111, 114, 115, 124, 125, 134, 135
Wright, G G, 140, 141
Wright, George G, 54, 55, 58, 59, 66, 67, 70, 71, 74, 75, 78, 79, 82, 83, 88, 89, 100, 101, 108, 109, 114, 115, 120, 121, 124, 125, 130, 131, 134, 135, 144, 145
Wright, Henry, 144, 145, 154, 155
Wright, James, 16, 17, 20, 40, 41, 44, 45, 48, 49, 54, 55, 58, 59, 66, 67, 70, 71, 74, 75, 78, 79, 82, 83, 88, 89, 90, 91, 94, 95, 102, 103, 108, 109, 114, 115, 120, 121, 126, 127, 134, 135, 140, 141, 144, 145, 150, 151, 154, 155, 158, 159, 164, 165, 170, 171, 174, 175, 176, 177, 178, 179, 180, 181, 187, 188, 189, 190, 191, 192, 200, 201, 202, 207, 208, 209, 214, 215, 216, 227, 228, 229
Wright, Jas, 2, 8, 24, 25, 26, 27, 28, 29, 30, 31, 32, 33, 34, 35, 36, 37, 200, 201, 202, 210, 211, 212
Wright Senr, Jas, 3
Wright, Jesse, 8, 13, 16, 21, 31, 32, 33, 34, 35, 363, 37, 40, 41, 44, 45, 48, 49, 54, 55, 58, 59, 66, 67, 70, 71, 74, 75, 78, 79, 84, 85, 88, 89, 100, 101, 111, 114, 115, 120, 121, 124, 125, 130, 131, 136, 137, 150, 151, 154, 155, 162,

163, 168, 169, 174, 175, 176, 177, 187, 188, 189, 204, 205, 206, 220, 221, 222, 237
Wright Jr., Jesse, 96, 97
Wright Senr, Jesse, 96, 97
Wright, Jessee, 3, 158, 159, 200, 201, 202, 227, 228, 229, 238, 239
Wright, Jno, 2, 8, 17, 20, 24, 25, 26, 27, 28, 29, 30, 48, 49
Wright SR, Jno, 40, 41
Wright (SR), Jno, 17, 31, 32, 33, 34, 35, 36, 37
Wright (SR), Jono., 8
Wright, John, 12, 20, 21, 40, 41, 44, 45, 48, 49, 54, 55, 58, 59, 62, 63, 66, 67, 70, 71, 74, 75, 78, 79, 82, 83, 88, 89, 994, 95, 100, 101, 108, 109, 114, 115, 124, 125, 126, 127, 134, 135, 140, 141, 154, 155, 158, 159
Wright, John B, 104, 105, 108, 109, 120, 121, 124, 125, 130, 131, 134, 135, 144, 145, 150, 151, 154, 155, 158, 159, 164, 165, 168, 169, 174, 175, 176, 177, 184, 185, 186, 194, 195, 196, 204, 205, 206, 214, 215, 216, 224, 225, 226, 234, 235, 236
Wright, John R., 114, 115
Wright, John W, 140, 141
Wright, Joseph A, 194, 195, 196
Wright, Landon, 13, 40, 41
Wright, Lucy, 48, 49, 58, 59, 66, 67, 74, 75, 78, 79, 82, 83, 88, 89, 96, 97, 110, 111, 116, 117
Wright, Lunden, 74, 75
Wright, Margret, 48, 49
Wright, Mary, 237, 238, 239
Wright, Moses, 3, 9, 13, 16, 224, 225, 226
Wright, Nancy, 197, 198, 199, 204, 205, 206, 220, 221, 222, 227, 228, 229, 237, 238, 239
Wright, Nelson, 17, 20, 31, 32, 33, 34, 35, 36, 37, 40, 41, 54, 55, 58, 59, 74, 75, 78, 79, 84, 85, 88, 89, 94, 95, 100, 101, 108, 109, 116,

117, 120, 121, 124, 125, 130, 131, 134, 135, 140, 141, 146, 147, 150, 151, 164, 165, 168, 169, 174, 175, 176, 177, 184, 185, 186, 194, 195, 196, 210, 211, 212, 216, 217, 218, 219, 230, 231, 232, 237, 238, 239
Wright, Parmenos, 13, 20
Wright, Permenos, 9
Wright, Richard, 234, 235, 236
Wright, Ro., 17, 24, 25, 26, 27, 28, 29, 30
Wright, Robert, 8, 12, 20, 154, 155, 168, 169, 207, 208, 209, 224, 225, 226, 237, 238, 239
Wright, Robert K, 207, 208, 209, 222, 224, 225, 226, 234, 235, 236, 220, 221
Wright, Robert M, 144, 145, 162, 163, 174, 175, 176, 177, 187, 188, 189, 194, 195, 196, 204, 205, 206, 214, 215, 216, 224, 225, 226, 234, 235, 236
Wright, Robt, 2
Wright, Samuel B, 158, 159, 168, 169, 178, 179, 180, 181, 184, 185, 1886, 197, 198, 199, 204, 205, 206
Wright, Shelton, 82, 83, 88, 89, 94, 95, 110, 111, 114, 115, 124, 125, 140, 141, 150, 151, 154, 155, 158, 159, 162, 163, 170, 171, 174, 175, 176, 177, 184, 185, 186, 197, 198, 199, 207, 208, 209
Wright, Thomas F, 170, 171
Wright, Thomas P, 158, 159, 162, 163
Wright, Thos, 16, 21
Wright, Westley, 48, 49
Wright, Wiatt, 90, 91
Wright, William, 12, 13, 44, 45, 54, 55, 58, 59, 62, 63, 66, 67, 70, 71, 74, 75, 78, 79, 82, 83, 88, 89, 90, 91, 94, 95, 100, 101, 154, 155, 158, 159, 194, 195, 196
Wright (JR), William, 154, 155
Wright Junr, William, 82, 83
Wright Senr, William, 58, 59, 96, 97
Wright, William B, 70, 71, 90, 91, 94, 95, 104, 105
Wright, William H, 158, 159, 162, 163, 168, 169, 187, 188, 189, 194, 195, 196, 224, 225, 226, 237, 238, 239
Wright, William R, 158, 159, 162, 163, 170, 171, 174, 175, 176, 177, 187, 188, 189
Wright, Wm, 16, 20,m 21, 24, 25, 26, 27, 28, 29, 30, 40, 41, 48, 49, 108, 109, 116, 117, 120, 121, 126, 127, 130, 131, 134, 135, 140, 141, 146, 147, 150, 151
Wright Snr, Wm, 124, 125
Wright, Wm B, 108, 109, 130, 131, 134, 135, 144, 145, 114, 115
Wright, Wm R, 124, 125, 130, 131, 134, 135, 140, 141, 144, 145, 150, 151
Wright, Wm., 2
Wright, Wyatt, 90, 91, 94, 95, 100, 1001, 110, 111

Other Heritage Books by Robert N. Grant

Identifying the Wrights in the Goochland County, Virginia Tithe Lists, 1732-84

The Identification of 1809 William Wright of Franklin County, Virginia, as the Son of 1792 John Wright of Fauquier County, Virginia, and Elizabeth (Bronaugh) (Darnall) Wright

Wright Family Birth Records (1853-1896) and Marriage Records (1788-1915): Franklin County, Virginia, 1853-1896

Wright Family Birth Records, 1853-1896; Marriage Records, 1761-1900; Census Records, 1810-1900, in Amherst County, Virginia

Wright Family Birth Records, 1853-1896; Marriage Records, 1808-1910; Census Records, 1810-1900; Patent Deeds and Land Grants; Deed Records, 1808-1910; Death Records, 1853-1896; Probate Records, 1808-1900, in Nelson County, Virginia

Wright Family Birth Records (1853-1896) and Marriage Records (1782-1900): Campbell County, Virginia

Wright Family Birth Records, Marriage Records, and Personal Property Tax Lists: Appomattox County, Virginia

Wright Family Census Records, Deed Records, Land Tax Lists, Death Records and Probate Records: Appomattox County, Virginia

Wright Family Census Records: Bedford County, Virginia, 1810-1900

Wright Family Census Records: Campbell County, Virginia, 1810-1900

Wright Family Census Records: Franklin County, Virginia, 1810-1900

Wright Family Death Records (1853-1920), Cemetery Records by Cemetery, and Probate Records (1782-1900): Campbell County, Virginia

Wright Family Death Records (1854-1920), Cemetery Records by Cemetery, and Probate Records (1785-1928): Franklin County, Virginia

Wright Family Death, Cemetery and Probate Records: Bedford County, Virginia

Wright Family Deed Records (1782-1900) and Land Tax List (1782-1850): Campbell County, Virginia

Wright Family Land Grants (1785-1900) and Deed Records (1785-1897): Franklin County, Virginia

Wright Family Land Grants, Deed Records, Land Tax List, Death Records, Probate Records: Prince Edward County, Virginia

Wright Family Land Records: Bedford County, Virginia

Wright Family Land Tax Lists: Franklin County, Virginia, 1786-1860

Wright Family Land Tax Records: Amherst County, Virginia, 1782-1850

Wright Family Land Tax Records: Nelson County, Virginia, 1809-1850

Wright Family Patent Deeds and Land Grants, 1761-1900, Deed Records, 1761-1903; Chancery Court Files, 1804-1900; Death Records, 1853-1920; Cemetery Records by Cemetery; and Probate Records, 1761-1900, in Amherst County, Virginia

Wright Family Personal Property Tax Lists: Amherst County, Virginia, 1782-1850

Wright Family Personal Property Tax Lists: Campbell County, Virginia, 1785-1850

Wright Family Personal Property Tax Lists: Franklin County, Virginia, 1786-1850

Wright Family Personal Property Tax Lists: Nelson County, Virginia, 1809-1850

Wright Family Personal Property Tax Records for Bedford County, Virginia, 1782 to 1850

Wright Family Records: Births in Bedford County, Virginia

Wright Family Records: Land Tax List, Bedford County, Virginia, 1782-1850

Wright Family Records: Lynchburg, Virginia Birth Records (1853-1896), Marriage Records (1805-1900), Marriage Notices (1794-1880), Census Records (1900), Deed Records (1805-1900), Death Records (1853-1896), Probate Records (1805-1900)

Wright Family Records: Marriages in Bedford County, Virginia

Wright Family Records: Prince Edward County, Virginia Birth Records, Marriage Records, Election Polls, and Tithe List, Personal Property Tax List, Census